MarketplaceChristians.com

Devotions for Christians in the Workplace

Cheryl—
Thank you for your
words of love, and
encouragement..
Dr. Wendy Flint

Dr. Wendy Flint

Word Unlimited
Since 1985
Vancouver, WA
Indio, CA

MarketplaceChristians.com

Devotions for Christians in the Workplace

USA ISBN 978-0-9818470-0-9

Word Unlimited
World Wide Web: www.marketplacechristians.com
E-mail: doctorflint@yahoo.com

All scripture passages are from the Amplified Bible unless otherwise noted.

Printed in the United States of America

TABLE OF CONTENTS

Dedication

I dedicate this book to my husband, Terry Flint, who has always believed in me, always supported me, and always knew there was a calling on my life - even when I thought the calling was just my imagination.

Special Thanks

To Bev Peterson, a close friend, and Caroline Peterson, my God-daughter, who diligently edited the book in its final stages.

MarketplaceChristians.Com

The Lord has put on my heart to encourage Christians serving in the "marketplace." Marketplace is a term used to refer to the workplace. Webster defines marketplace as "the world of trade or economy" and "the everyday world." Jesus told us that we were to be in the world without being a part of the world. That is not always an easy calling and my desire is to encourage those that struggle in this century to find peace and balance in their life under the increased pressures of the marketplace.

Between 2003 and 2007 - I wrote over 250 devotions and e:mailed them to marketplace Christians. I have selected 157 of what I believe to be the best and the most encouraging messages for you. I love the number "57" because Psalm 57: 2 is what my life and this book is all about:

"I will cry to God Most High, Who performs on my behalf and rewards me. Who brings to pass His purposes for me and surly completes them!"

Dr. Wendy Flint

Introduction

On a rainy day in November, 1985, I had just returned home from the election returns after an exhausting day of calling people to get out the vote before the polls closed. I was lying on the couch in our modest home located in the low-income area of the school district. The 10-o'clock news was on and my face appeared on the screen being interviewed by a news reporter.

I had just won a controversial school board election with 53% of the vote in the 10th largest school district in the state of Washington. I jumped from the couch, ran to the bathroom, curled up in a corner and began to uncontrollably sob, holding my stomach.

What had I done? The excitement of the campaign was over and now I had to face the responsibility of school board leadership with thousands of people watching me. I was described as "a mother in pigtails" by Christians and a "right-wing radical" by the press. After ten years of serving as a volunteer in my children's schools, I only thought of myself as a mother.

I didn't have a degree, I held no profession, except daycare provider, and I was extremely insecure as a female in leadership. I ran my campaign on a shoestring budget of donations and I had no finances for fancy clothes or hairdos. My only credentials were that I obeyed God, ran the race, faced persecution, and won.

There was no celebration with relatives; I had very few friends of support; my children were unhappy with me because of the rejection they received from students and teachers; and my husband, a quiet man, was still shell-shocked from all the newspaper and television coverage. It felt very much like a bitter-sweet victory.

I sat on the bathroom floor, alone, scared, and unprepared. In that moment of despair, the doorbell rang. A Christian man I barely knew who pounded "Wendy Flint" signs in yards for months, sent me flowers with a note, "You are beautiful. God loves you. Thank you."

With that note of encouragement, I took a deep breath, prayed, and began my journey of leadership with the Lord.

That journey from 1985 to 2008, took me through multiple job descriptions and degrees, as I became an author, professor, national speaker, and corporate executive.

Even though I had learning disabilities, God called me back to school and from age 44 to age 54, I earned three degrees, receiving my doctorate in June 2004 becoming Dr. Wendy Flint. I leaned my entire personality on the Lord Jesus Christ to overcome my fears to reach these goals. It is this "leaning" and learning that became my messages in this book.

My desire and purpose is to increase the hope, love, faith, joy, and peace of my fellow sisters and brothers in the Lord who may wonder, "what possible plan could God have for my life in the workplace?"

Take heart, my friends. In these last days, He has a GREAT PLAN to use you.

Preface

I think back to why I started doing this project of writing daily messages for Christians in the workplace and I recall I simply had a desire to meet the spiritual need of fellow workers.

I was working at a college campus for four years when, in 2003, I finally located other Christians that worked at the college. Several were invited to a lunch by a long-time employee of the school district to hear my personal testimony and that lunch led to a weekly lunch-hour Bible study.

At the end of the school year, May 2003, many attended a National Day of Prayer presentation in the school theatre, organized by the Student Christian Club. At the National Day of Prayer, I saw many other employees in attendance. Several asked me as the faculty advisor for the Student Christian Club to please organize other events to encourage them and I sensed their weariness and great need for fellowship.

At the beginning of the Fall semester, September 2003, I tried to organize another weekly prayer and Bible study. We could not find a common day or time to meet and most people only had a half-hour for lunch with no flexibility. I was very discouraged. I prayed, "God show me what I can do to encourage these people that work so hard in the marketplace - they need Your love." The Lord impressed on my heart, "Use e-mail to write to them." I shared with several people and they agreed with the concept, using home e-mail addresses.

By September 21, 2003, I sent my first devotion. A half-dozen readers at the college soon grew to thirty recipients off campus. Later in the year, my Biola University (Bible Institute of Los Angeles) students were reading them. By September 2004, one year later, 150 Christians throughout California, Washington, and Oregon were on the distribution list and they were forwarding them to friends and relatives throughout the nation.

By 2008, over 250 people from multiple companies and organizations were receiving the daily messages with no advertising on my part. It wasn't until I received a message from a military woman who was facing the aftermath of Katrina in New Orleans, that I realized how they were reaching marketplace Christians beyond "my borders" giving wisdom and strength to those in need.

In February 2006, a pastor who had successfully published several books, contacted publishing companies hoping they would find interest in my writings. The response was, "We don't print devotionals anymore unless the person is famous because there is no demand for them."

Rather than be discouraged, I set about to self-publish. The testimonies coming to me indicated that the Holy Spirit was working powerfully through the messages and I knew they needed to reach others in the marketplace.

I believe the many struggles I endured over the years regarding getting this book published was because the final book would set captives free from their personal limitations or fears. I was determined to not give up. A year later, in February 2007, I finished editing the devotions and even found a renewed strength to write a few more. I decided to sort them in categories of themes that had emerged and with the help of a dear friend, finalized the edits and scripture references by May 2008.

From 2003 to 2008, I obeyed God and continued to work on this book, usually very early in the morning before I went to work. My desire was always to be up in a cabin in the woods writing with no distractions, but it was God's will that I was working in the marketplace as the messages came forth.

The book is in God's hands now. May the Holy Spirit strengthen you and give you wisdom in your calling, whether a leader of your home or a leader in the workplace, through the words I have written for you. My journey has been through politics, non-profit organizations, K-12 education, higher education, government, and multiple corporations.

I have walked where you are. There is a message in this book for every person in the Marketplace.

Part 1
Pursuing Excellence

Payday

With what judgment you judge, you will be judged; and with the measure you use, it will be measured back to you.

Matthew 7:2 NKJV

The measuring rod you use on others will be the same one that measures you. This is not because God is into retaliation, but because He put a law in place that 1) will not change, and 2) will work for good or bad for us like every other law.

"Give and it shall be given unto you" and "you will reap what you sow" are not just Biblical slogans. They are standards that can give us an abundant life if we obey them. The same is true about Romans 2:1: "For in posing as judge and passing sentence on another, you condemn yourself."

This topic is a very personal one between you and God.

It requires taking a searchlight in our hearts to see if we are judging others. Jesus said, "Blessed are the merciful, for they shall receive mercy" (Matthew 5:7, NASB).

When someone is going through a challenge we do not understand, it is very dangerous and arrogant to think we are somehow better or more spiritual. If we do judge too harshly, God may allow us to go through the same thing to develop mercy and compassion in us. Romans 2:1 also says, that people who habitually judge, "are habitually practicing the very same things that (they) censure and denounce."

In the 1960's I was given an illegal "black box" that allowed me to make free long distance calls. In the 1970's, the Holy Spirit began to show me that I was stealing from the phone company. Under the conviction of the Lord, I prayed, "God, if you really want me to give that to the phone company and risk criminal charges, I will, but you will have to bring a phone truck to my house to convince me, because I'm afraid."

I opened the curtains after breakfast, and there at the curb was a phone truck! I walked out to the curb and handed it to the technician.

She was in shock. "Do you know what this is?" she exclaimed. And then she asked, "Why are you giving this to me?"

I shared with her my relationship with Jesus Christ and His desire for me to be honest. She shook her head in disbelief.

Today, when I see people stealing things I start to get judgmental and have to catch myself and remember that I hold within me the same ability to sin. God does not want us to be that man or woman at the altar that says, "I'm so glad I don't live like those heathens do, and that I am righteous before God."

Rather, He desires us to say, "I am so unworthy and do not deserve your mercy and love."

To the first one, Jesus will say, "I know you not." To the second one, Jesus will say, "Enter into the kingdom of heaven my good and faithful servant." In all the decisions we make, we need to think about the final payday.

The Traffic Free Mile

Let patience have her perfect work, that ye may be perfect and entire, wanting nothing.

James 1:4 KJV

The book of James instructs us to consider it joyful when we encounter trails of any sort. Why? Because "the trial and proving of your faith bring out endurance and steadfastness and patience" (v. 3).

Without trials, we will never be fully developed. When we fail countless times, we see it as failure, but God sees it as marathon training.

We are learning how to walk; He picks us up when we fall down; eventually we are running; and someday we are marathon material. God is a patient God and He is asking us to allow His patient work to take place in our lives.

James took over the leadership of the Jerusalem church after Peter left Palestine. He presided at the Jerusalem council where the church leaders reached an agreement for the basis of Christian fellowship.

This man of God has my attention – he is a respected church leader and a great meeting facilitator. James was concerned with the practical and ethical life of Christians.

He believed that a genuine faith must produce good works, or what I call a (spirit of excellence). He was very familiar with Jesus' teachings, was present on the Day of Pentecost, and he sought to preserve the *Sermon on the Mount.*

James did not like religious hypocrisy. He had an irritation with Christians who would tell a poor person "I'll pray for you" in lieu of giving him food and clothing.

James was unwavering in his faith, and he tells us, if you want wisdom, then ask for it. Obviously, he had first hand experience with this concept.

James is a short book, but a powerful book on principled and practical Christianity and leadership. James would have liked the leadership teachings of Zig Ziglar: "There's no traffic jam on the extra mile."

Leadership author John C. Maxwell comments along these same lines: "If you always do more than is expected, not only will you rise up above the crowd, you will help others to rise up with you."

James, Ziglar, and Maxwell are telling us to be good Christian examples; and that in the workplace and in leadership we need to give our all as unto the Lord.

Workplace Beatitudes

Blessed are...

Matthew 5: 3-11

Some people believe that the *Sermon on the Mount* sums up everything Jesus wanted to say to us and that it is the greatest sermon ever preached. After studying the *Sermon on the Mount,* I've rewritten it to apply to our modern-day workplace:

Blessed are employees who work for God and do not get any earthly recognition, but continue to do their jobs well, for theirs is the kingdom of heaven and their reward is in heaven (3).

Blessed are those that cry over difficult bosses or co-workers, do not get the promotion, long for a better job, or lose their job, for they shall be comforted (and the Lord will care for them) (4).

Blessed are those that have a servant-leader attitude and are willing to do even the lowest task to get the job done, for they shall inherit the earth (5).

Blessed are those that hunger after God's Word, seek His direction, depend on Him, and put their lives in His hands, for they shall be filled with His Spirit, His Strength, and His Wisdom (6).

Blessed are those that forgive others that hurt, betray, ignore, or take advantage of those in the workplace, for they shall obtain mercy when they make mistakes themselves (7).

Blessed are those that have a pure heart and only think the best of others, believe in others, hope for others, pray for others, and serve others, for they shall see God and experience His presence and hear Him say, "Well done, my good and faithful servant; you represented Me well" (8).

Blessed are the peacemakers that seek to bring resolution in conflict, who stand for what is right, and who help to protect the feelings of others, for they shall be called the children of God (9).

Blessed are they which are persecuted when they ethically stand for what is right and refuse to participate in wrongdoing, even if it means the loss of a job or loss of favor, for theirs is the kingdom of heaven and they shall have great reward on earth and in heaven (10).

Blessed are you (I believe that Jesus changed from third to the first person, because at this point, He looked at His disciples) when men shall revile you, and persecute you, and shall say all manner of evil against you falsely, for my sake (11). Amen.

Faithful in the Small Things

For this very reason, adding your diligence (to the divine promises), employ every effort in exercising your faith to develop virtue (excellence, resolution, Christian energy), and in (exercising) virtue (develop) knowledge.

2 Peter 1: 5

Peter offers one of my favorite lessons in the Bible, because the theme is knowledge. The words "know" and "knowledge" occur more than sixteen times in this epistle, and there is a focus on character building and the development of "the divine nature" in our daily lives.

Peter tells us that if we employ every effort to develop virtue (excellence) that in turn will develop knowledge and intelligence (v. 5). If we exercise knowledge and develop self-control, steadfastness, and endurance, that in turn will develop godliness (v. 6). If we exercise godliness and develop brotherly affection, that in turn will develop our ultimate goal – Christian love (v. 7).

Peter says if we work at having these qualities abound in us, they will keep us from being idle or unfruitful (v. 8). If we are not focused on building our character, we become lazy and disobedient. It is very clear to me that all of this begins with "attitude."

Work ethic for God, for our families, or for our workplace begins in our hearts. I call it "a spirit of excellence."

We need to desire to serve God with excellence in small things to achieve excellence in big things. The Bible says about Daniel that there was "a spirit of excellence upon him."

Through obedience, Daniel took steps to serve God in the small things, and later God honored him with large responsibilities. One of my favorite expressions is, "That person is so super spiritual he is no earthly good." God wants us to have "earthly good" in the common things.

Peter said we should "give all diligence" on forming godly habits. The grace of God that gives us miracles in times of great challenges is the same grace that builds character through our common everyday tasks.

Daniel's life was not only dreams and visions and the lion's den experience. As governor of the land, he faced the daily tasks of paper pushing, project management, government red tape, jealous co-workers, and people conflicts. He prayed on his knees at least three times a day to honor God and to receive from Him grace and strength, character building, wisdom, and direction.

There are no shortcuts to leadership success. Whatever assignments God gives you, do it with excellence. If you are faithful in the small things, He will give you more.

Stale Water

He refused to drink it; instead, he poured it out before the Lord.
2 Samuel 23:16

Water that does not flow becomes dead, stagnant, and stale, and it stinks. If we do not pour out our life for the Lord, the same can happen to us.

In the marketplace, we have plenty of opportunities to pour out our blessings, our love, and our time. John Maxwell, author of *Life @ Work,* writes that Jesus calls you and me to be "Everyday Samaritans." The Samaritan story can be found in Luke 10: 30 – 37.

Referring to the Samaritan who helped the man who was attacked by robbers, Jesus said, "Go and do the same," and He tells us to "love your neighbor as yourself."

Maxwell answers the question, "Who exactly qualifies as my neighbor?" He writes: "My neighbor is anyone that crosses my path and who needs help that I can afford to provide." Examples he gives are taking the next plane to give a member of a family trying to get to a wedding a seat, scrambling to meet a client's eleventh-hour demand, helping someone in the parking lot jump start a dead battery, pulling over to assist in an accident, or helping a client on something for which you do not get commission.

In 2005, I went to a brother-in-the-Lord who works in a marketing firm. I told him I needed help with the sales of an educational program. I stated right up front that my employer could not afford to pay anything and that the best I could do was to let others know about his firm.

I shared that I had tried everything, and I was worried about the success of the program. I asked if he would help me with just a few suggestions.

He not only gave me a list of ideas, he sent me a mock-up of an ad copy that he thought would work, and he sends me occasional e-mails at work with new marketing concepts. He went way beyond what I expected and blessed me.

To do the vision that God called me to, I needed help, and he helped me. To my brother I would like to say, "I will pass it forward and help someone else," and "I pray for rivers of life to continue to flow through your life."

Maximum Capacity

Stay here and keep watch with Me.

Matthew 26:38 NLT

Are you giving Jesus your maximum capacity? Or do you fall asleep when you enter into prayer or spiritual warfare because of your own natural limitations? Do you seek help from God first, or as a last resort?

In the Garden of Gethsemane, the disciples fell asleep instead of praying with Jesus. A short time later, when He was arrested, they all fled. After the ascension of Jesus, these formerly fearful men transformed into bold witnesses for the kingdom of God.

What changed in their lives? Jesus told them, "You will receive power when the Holy Spirit comes upon you …" (Acts 1:8, NASB). Then in Acts 2:4, "They were all filled with the Holy Spirit" (KJV).

To serve Jesus at our maximum capacity, we must receive the guidance of the Holy Spirit and be open to His wisdom and teaching. God also desires that we be at our maximum capacity in the workplace or He would not have pointed out to us that Daniel "was excellent in all he did."

A national best selling secular business book, *Good to Great,* by Jim Collins, offers some research results. Collins confirms that getting the "right" people on board with a project or company is the key to success. Trying to train the "wrong people" is doomed to failure.

Who are the right people? Disciplined people who apply disciplined thought and action.

What else did Collins discover about great companies? They embraced an unwavering faith that they can and will prevail in the end, regardless of the difficulties, and at the same time have the discipline to confront the most brutal facts of current reality.

Why do you think secular kings promoted Joseph, Nehemiah, Esther, and Daniel into high positions of authority? They were disciplined, gave maximum capacity to their organizations or personal mission, they had faith to prevail, and they depended on prayer to guide them in their decision-making.

Collins asks the question, "What creates enduring great organizations?" His research concludes, "enduring great people."

Excellence means both using all the skills and talents the Lord gives us to the best of our ability and depending on Him completely. In order to live disciplined lives for God and for our organizations, we need to let God have control.

In the book, *God is My CEO,* author Larry Julian notes that the most important relationship the successful CEO's had was the private, ongoing, daily relationship with the Lord. The first step in each CEO's decision was to seek God's wisdom. Why don't you team-up with the Holy Spirit to get the job done?

Our Best for His Glory

We have renounced secret and shameful ways …

2 Corinthians 4:2 NIV

The Amplified version of this Scripture is powerful: "We have renounced disgraceful ways (secret thoughts, feelings, desires and underhandedness, the methods and arts that men hide through shame); we refuse to deal craftily (to practice trickery and cunning) or to adulterate or handle dishonestly the Word of God, but we state openly (clearly and candidly). And so we commend ourselves in the sight and presence of God to every man's conscience."

Any envy, jealousy, strife, dishonesty, or resentment in which we participated in the past, must be renounced as it comes to the surface. If we suppress these things, rather than renounce these things in a quick prayer, we will dull the spirit and lose our motivation for God.

Because of my zeal for God, my passion for Christ, and my desire to live totally for Him, it is embarrassing for me to hear that some people think I am some sort of super spiritual or religious person. I AM NOT! I am a "confessed person."

I came to God in confession of my sins, and I walk with God in confession and in renouncement of anything that would try to raise itself up against God's truth. It is my desire that all would understand that it is all about God in us – it is *not about us.*

When a Christian begins to believe that somehow they have a better walk or relationship with God than someone else – that is when religion and judgment take over. A relationship with God is simply allowing God to remove your old sin nature and to form you into a higher standard for Him.

Religion is taking those standards and holding other people up to them. That is not what Christ intended. It is about giving our best for His Glory (not ours).

The Kingdom of God Is at Hand

May you experience the love of Christ, though it is too great to understand fully. Then you will be made complete with all the fullness of life and power that comes from God.

Ephesians 3:19 NLT

Jesus often said, "The kingdom of God is at hand!" He was talking about the energy, power, and grace of God that is available through Jesus here on earth.

We look forward to eternal life in heaven, but we can also have the eternal life that Jesus Christ exhibited on the human level. Many Christians say, "If having an eternal home in heaven was the only thing I received from Jesus, I would be satisfied no matter how bad it is here on earth."

But Jesus wanted so much more for us. He overcame the world so that we could experience God on earth and not wait until we arrived in heaven. He wants us to experience the fullness of God.

Jesus wants us to apply kingdom principles through faith to our finances, our marriages, our children, and our work situations. He does not intend for us to live with the status quo.

Jesus repeatedly told people, "The kingdom of God is at hand!" He wanted them to know that they could experience heaven on earth. Try walking into your workplace today and proclaiming (before everyone else arrives), "The kingdom of God is at hand!"

Invite the kingdom of God into your home, into your marriage, into your job, into your finances, into the leadership of your church, into the government of this country, and into this world.

Following is Psalm 23 rewritten for the workplace:

Psalm 23

(Author Unknown)

> The Lord is my real boss, and I shall not want.
> He gives me peace, when chaos is all around me.
> He gently reminds me to pray

And do all things without murmuring and complaining.
He reminds me that HE (and not my job) is my source.
He restores my sanity everyday

And guides my decisions

That I might honor him in all that I do.
Even though I face an absurd amount of e-mails, system crashes,
Unrealistic deadlines, budget cutbacks, gossiping co-workers,
And an aging body that doesn't cooperate
Every morning, I still will not stop - for He is with me!
His presence, His peace, and His power will see me through.
He raises me up, even when they fail to promote me.
He claims me as His own,

Even when the company threatens to let me go.
His faithfulness and love are better than any bonus check.
His retirement plan beats every 401k there is!
When it's all said and done,

I'll be working for Him a whole lot longer
And for that, I bless His name!

The Extra Mile

Whoever compels you to go one mile, go with him two.
Matthew 5:41 NKJV

The Good Samaritan in this story gave his time and money to a robbed and beaten man. In telling this parable, Jesus said that the Good Samaritan instructed the innkeeper to keep a tab of the cost to care for the assaulted man and that he would take care of the entire debt.

In the *Sermon on the Mount,* Jesus said if a soldier commands you to carry something one mile, go with him two miles. We cannot do that with our own natural tendency. Only through Jesus Christ within us can we go the extra mile. It is only through God's supernatural grace that we are made disciples of Jesus.

After having my car broken into near where I live, I discovered my purse and cell phone stolen. The window replacement was $169.

The incident revealed a negative attitude within me that God wanted to deal with. I was angry at the selfishness and evil that made what I pictured to be a young man who did this (I figured he was young because it was in a high school parking lot, and he had to jump through a small back window quickly).

I was trying to figure out how people can live with a guilty conscience about these things. My husband said, "If they are on drugs, they don't feel anything."

God brought to my mind and heart my anger towards this person and said, "Here is an opportunity for you to pray for your enemy." Since I do not want anything to separate me from my walk with God, I not only forgave this person, I began to pray for his soul and salvation through Jesus Christ. I prayed until I had the compassion of Jesus for a hurting person who was living a life of crime.

The city I live in has a high crime rate. When the crime happened to me, I cried out in the parking lot that day in frustration, "I hate this city! I don't want to live here anymore!"

John Maxwell writes, "It is impossible to be truly converted to God without being thereby converted to our neighbor." The people in this city are my neighbors, including the youth who committed this crime, and God says I must be committed to them in prayer.

James 2:15-16 in a modern translation of the Bible says, "God-talk without God-acts is outrageous nonsense."

Dear Lord, Open up our hearts to show us how you want us to go the extra mile in our cities and with our neighbors. In Jesus' name, we pray. Amen.

Even in the Small Things

Do all things without grumbling and faultfinding and complaining (against God) and questioning and doubting (among yourselves).
Philippians 2:14

On our 35th wedding anniversary (2004), my husband and I went to Gettysburg, Pennsylvania. While in Gettysburg, I visited with the Christian owner, age 54 and in a wheelchair, of the bed-and-breakfast where we stayed.

At age 52, she had a sudden brain infection, and it paralyzed the entire left side of her body. She went from actively operating a business to dependence on her husband to do everything.

I asked her if she had learned anything through her circumstances that she could share with me. She said, "People complain too much."

She went on to explain that her church had made arrangements for a different person each week to pick her up and drive her to church. In her paralyzed state, she was "locked" in the car with them and forced to listen.

She said, "People whine and complain about the smallest things. For example, they complain about how they are getting old, they share all their little petty aches and pains, as if somehow they were supposed to escape that stage of their life!" She continued, " people need to express more gratitude. "

Here is a woman whose life as she once knew it had ended. Her lesson to us is, "be more grateful." She also added, "I pray more. I can't do much of anything else, so I spend most of my day praying for others."

Most of us find it easy to keep the Lord's commandments in the big things. We do not cheat, lie, or steal. It is in the little things that we forget what He requires of us. Jesus said, "If anyone desires to come after Me, let him deny himself . . ." (Luke 9:23, NKJV).

How about the "small" instructions that Jesus gave us to quit worrying about what we wear or what we will eat. Paul wrote to the Philippians, "(Be) content with (your) earthly lot of whatever sort that is, (and that peace) which transcends all understanding shall garrison and mount guard over your hearts and MINDS in Christ Jesus" (Philippians 4:7).

Paul then writes to only think on "whatever is true... noble... right... pure... lovely... admirable... excellent... worthy of praise" (Philippians 4:8, NIV).

The Israelites got stuck in the wilderness for 40 years, because of a very small thing – whining and complaining. God will flow through your praises and your positive attitude – He cannot flow through grumbling and depression.

So what do you do with the reality of life? "In every circumstance and in everything, by prayer and petition (definite requests), with thanksgiving, continue to make your wants known to God" (Philippians 4:6).

Willing to Look Foolish

Whether you eat, or drink, or whatever you do, do all to the glory of God.
1 Corinthians 10:31 NIV

Jesus lived among the everyday people and participated in everyday events. In the book *Jesus CEO,* author, Laurie Beth Jones points out how some of the greatest Biblical characters had to appear shallow and "non-profound."

Noah appeared to be a "deluded engineer." Moses, turning water into blood, was called a "magician." Nehemiah actually started out as a waiter (a cupbearer to a king) and then boldly asked to cut down a forest to build a wall. Queen Esther was a member of a harem. Mary conceived a child before marriage. And Jesus was called a blasphemer.

What did all of these saints have in common? They were willing to be foolish for God and didn't care what other people thought. More importantly, God USED THEM in the everyday functions of life, and they demonstrated God's power and their own personal, childlike faith through obedience, not through proclaiming profound mysteries of God.

Laurie Beth Jones writes: "Jesus was willing to look foolish. And this was the key to his success. Coming into town on a donkey, having to fish to pay your taxes, and forgetting to bring the wine do not seem like ingredients for success. Omega leaders cannot be afraid to look foolish. We must keep to the plan that we vaguely sense but that only God can see."

When God asks you to do something that seems shallow, unimportant, and not profound, remember the words of Jesus: "what you do for the least of these, you do for me."

When God asks you to do something that is going to cause people to talk about you, judge you, or persecute you, remember Isaiah 41: 10: "Fear not, for I am with you; be not dismayed, for I am your God. I will strengthen you, yes, I will help you, I will uphold you with my righteous right hand."

Does it seem foolish what God is calling you to do? Does it seem shallow or mundane? Then He must have a special call on your life.

Be of great joy today and be thankful for the marketplace ministry He has given you. Like Nehemiah, you are building "spiritual walls" for God's Kingdom.

Keep Your Eyes on Jesus

Behold, as the eyes of servants look to the hand of their master… so our eyes look to the Lord our God.

Psalm 123:2

How many times have we been told as Christians to "keep our eyes on Jesus" without fully understanding what that means. Laurie Beth Jones points out in *Jesus CEO* that Jesus "met with his boss daily, usually for hours," and nothing interrupted that time.

Jones, an experienced corporate executive, writes, "Chances are your boss (Jesus) can provide an aerial view that will make your path more clear." She asks the question, "How regularly do you communicate with your boss?"

Bruce Wilkinson in *Secrets of the Vine* tells his readers, "God's purpose is not that you will do more for Him, but that you will choose to be more with Him." Jesus said, "As the branch cannot bear fruit of itself, except it abide in the Vine; no more can ye, except ye abide in Me" (John 15:4, KJV)

Do you sense a spiritual leak in your life? Are your grape vines not bearing any fruit? Recognize that something has been coming between you and God, and get it readjusted at once. Do not let Satan keep you away from Jesus for another minute.

Jesus said, "I am the vine, you are the branches. He who abides in Me, and I in him, bears much fruit; for without me you can do nothing" (John 15:5, NKJV).

Here are suggestions on how you can abide with Jesus:

- Set aside a special time with God, perhaps early in the morning.
- Read the Bible as if it is a love letter from God to you.
- Apply what you read in the Bible to your present circumstances.
- Talk to Him like you would a friend.
- Take time to be still before Him.

- Seek Him until you find Him.

- Keep a daily written record of what God is doing in your life – a spiritual journal. Share with Him your disappointments, celebrations, and confusions.

- Continue to obey him so you don't break the fellowship, but if you sin, repent immediately. Don't let a wedge of sin cut you off from fellowship with God.

- "Be strong in the Lord (be empowered through your UNION with Him); draw your strength from Him (that strength which His boundless might provides)" (Eph. 6:10). Keep looking up.

Habits

Do you not know that your body is the temple (the very sanctuary) of the Holy Spirit who lives within you, Whom you have received (as a gift) from God? You are not your own...

1 Corinthians 6: 19

God has given us the responsibility to rule over our own bodies and care for them. Daniel understood this concept when he turned down the king's rich food and chose instead to eat a healthy Hebrew diet. Daniel realized that God had an important plan for his life, and he would need to be healthy and strong in order to accomplish what God had set before him.

Whether it is smoking, overeating, drug addiction, laziness, or sexual lust, we need deliverance from bad habits. Paul says to pray in all things.

Germaine Copeland in *Prayers That Avail Much,* writes this prayer for habits:

Father, in the name of Jesus and according to Your Word, I believe in my heart and say with my mouth that Jesus is Lord of my life. Since all truth is in Jesus, I strip myself of my former nature. I desire to be free from the habit(s) of_____ in the name of Jesus. I no longer desire to be the slave of wrong habits and behaviors or be brought under their power. Father, these self-destructive habits are symptoms of a flaw in my soul, my character, and I confess them as sin. I don't want to habitually make the same mistakes over and over. Father, Your Word exposes the wrong thought patterns that are driving me to continue acting out in ways that are contrary to Your Word, I desire to be continually filled with, and controlled by the Holy Spirit. Amen

I used to struggle with high blood pressure and high blood sugar. I realized that I could not serve God or fulfill His purpose for life if I was physically ill or dead. I prayed for God to help me, but ultimately I had to help myself and be accountable to God with my temple. My blood pressure and blood sugar are now below normal as I work toward healthy eating and exercise.

All the rules, regulations, and requirements of the law concerning the body are summed up for me in this revealed truth – my body is "the temple of the Holy Spirit."

A Covenant Relationship

I have set my rainbow in the clouds, and it will be the sign of a covenant between Me and the earth.

Genesis 9:13 NIV

The first time I ever heard the word "covenant" was very early in my marriage and about two years after my husband Terry and I accepted the Lord Jesus Christ. We were going through a very difficult time emotionally and financially. In fact, it was so serious, we did not know if the marriage would make it.

We got down on our knees to pray to the Lord for His blessing and guidance. My husband said, "I heard the word 'covenant' – the Lord is making a covenant with us to keep us together." We had never heard that word before, so we looked it up.

"Covenant" in *Webster's Dictionary* means "a formal, solemn, and binding agreement; a written agreement or promise under seal between two or more parties for the performance of some action; to enter into a contract." We had such peace in that moment that we knew no matter what the circumstances, God was not only going to work on our behalf, He was also going to prevent the enemy from destroying our marriage.

The covenant will not work unless we participate in our part of the agreement. Many covenant promises in the Bible begin with, "If you only believe..." Our part of the covenant was to believe God's promise for our marriage.

I could list over 100 trials and heartaches that our marriage endured over the past years since we received that message, but we maintained our faith by holding to His promise in each and every situation, and God kept His covenant with us.

Are you waiting for God to fulfill a promise in your life, your ministry, or your workplace? Are you waiting for something to happen as evidence of God working instead of standing on faith in the covenant promise He has already given you? Faith believes in the promises of God, not in the feelings of something you have already received.

I once heard national speaker, Pastor Jessie Duplantis talk on faith.

He said that God is tired of having a bunch of "children" in the church. The Lord spoke to him in his heart and said, "Children are cute, and I love children, but it's time for my people to grow up and start activating their faith and standing on my Word. Children WAIT for things to come their way. Adults step out in faith and do their part."

Neither Cold Nor Hot

I know your (record of) works and what you are doing; you are neither cold nor hot.

Revelation 3:15

One of the most dangerous things we can do as a Christian is play games with God, trying to sit on a fence in order have a little of both worlds. In Revelation 3, Jesus spoke, in John's vision, to the Church of the Laodiceans and said, "I know your (record of works) and what you are doing; you are neither cold nor hot. Would that you were cold or hot! So, because you are neither cold nor hot, I will spew you out of My mouth!" (v. 15-16).

Just as you cannot have a little bit of sin in your life, you cannot have a little bit of Jesus. He wants you to give your all, or give nothing at all.

In the year 2001, I evaluated my life to see if I was completely "sold out" to Jesus. I had read in the Scripture that God rewards the faithful and that it is the faithful that abound.

I wanted to prosper physically and spiritually, so I looked closely at this word "faithful." I searched my heart and checked for the areas that I had been faithful and areas that I had been unfaithful.

I then asked for forgiveness and prayed for faith to follow through on the things I had been unfaithful in. On my faithful list were being a good mom and grandmother, persevering through difficult times in marriage, writing and encouraging my friends with Scripture, ministering to prisoners, forgiving others, and being obedient to God when He put challenging requests before me.

On my unfaithful list was my church attendance, praying for others everyday, tithing on a regular basis, and living in fear instead of trust when it came to money.

Does that surprise you? I was facing great challenges for God and working for His Kingdom, but I was unfaithful in the little. I quickly got "my house in order," and over the next few months; my opportunity to minister increased, the financial fear and bondage was broken off of me, and the fire came back into my relationship with Jesus.

Jesus concluded in his message to the Church of the Laodiceans, "Those whom I (dearly and tenderly) love, I tell their faults and convict and convince and reprove and chasten (I discipline and instruct them). So be enthusiastic and in earnest and burning with zeal and repent (changing your mind and attitude). Behold, I stand at the door and knock; if anyone hears and listens to and heeds My voice and opens the door, I will come in to him and will eat with him, and he (will eat) with Me" (Revelation 3:19-20).

Invite Jesus in today, and let Him bring a flashlight. Take communion with Him, and be prepared for a joyous, abundant life.

There Are No Shortcuts

*It is written that Abraham had two sons: the one by a bondwoman, the other
by a freewoman.*

Galatians 4:22 NKJV

If you try to take a shortcut off of the path that God has for your life,
you can go down that trail for awhile, but you will eventually come right
back to where you started. We all want to get from salvation to ministry,
from serving to leading, or from the dream to the fulfillment of the vision
overnight.

It does not happen that way. There are no shortcuts to God's spiritual
calling in our lives. The natural things that defy God must be dealt with
first, and we must also wait on God's perfect timing.

Abraham had a natural son by a bondwoman and then a spiritual son
(promised by God) by his wife. Abraham did not wait on God for the
promise and did it his own way. Millennia later, there are still wars
between the descendants of the bondwoman and the descendants of the
freewoman.

The Bible says we must lean our entire personality on God, yielding
to Him. I see so many Christians take their unyielding temperaments and
personalities into spiritual leadership. They skip the discipline of getting
their homes in order, their marriage secure, their tempers controlled, and
their children trained.

I am not saying everything has to be perfect to minister, but my
husband and I always watched with curiosity people staying late at the
church to practice for choir or fellowship with others while their children
were running around screaming, destroying property, or hitting other
children. There needs to be a balance between the time for spiritual
things and a time to take care of the natural responsibilities that God has
given us.

His Word is true today, just as it was 2,000 years ago – be faithful
over the little the Lord gives you, and He will give you more. Be faithful
in the natural things – faithful in the job he has given you, faithful with
the care of your home, faithful with the raising of your children, faithful

in your marriage, and be faithful in your giving. One day you will look over your shoulder and a wealth of physical and spiritual blessings will overtake you.

Kenneth Copeland gave his college-bound grandchildren the following advice for success: "If you are obedient today, you will be successful tomorrow. If you are obedient tomorrow, you will be successful the next day. If you are obedient next week, you will be successful the following week. If you are obedient each month, you will be successful at the end of the year."

Part 2
Purpose and Direction

Being Fully Persuaded

Jesus said to her, "Did I not say to you that if you would believe you would see the glory of God?"

John 11:40 NASB

The story in John 11 is the miracle of Jesus raising Lazarus from the dead. Martha and Mary, sisters to Lazarus, knew that Jesus was the Messiah, but when Jesus said, "I am the Resurrection and the Life and your brother shall rise again," they could not believe, because that did not make sense.

Commonsense is part of our natural life, but faith is part of our spiritual life. It is easy to believe what He tells us on the mountaintop, but when we come down to the valley of scoffers, it is difficult to maintain our faith.

That is why we have to put what God tells us in our "knower." We have to know that we know that we know that God told us to do something.

What we know will be tested, but we will survive the test with faith and perseverance. Everything that challenges our beliefs will strengthen our faith.

If you are fully persuaded in what God is telling you to do, then you should not turn back. In regards to Abraham having the promised son in his nineties, the Bible says, "No unbelief or distrust made him waiver, (doubtingly question) concerning the promise of God, but he grew strong and was empowered by faith as he gave praise and glory to God, fully satisfied and assured that God was able and mighty to keep His Word and do what He had promised" (Romans 4: 20-21).

I am fully persuaded that God is faithful; that He loves me, and I have entered a rest of knowing He will watch over me. I am fully persuaded that my life is completely in His hands.

I learned that we go through stages of faith from belief to knowledge to persuasion to commitment. There are people at each of these levels that are able to lift others up to the next level.

People in the believing stage are often storm tossed to-and-fro from believing to not believing as circumstances change. But once God gives someone a revelation and it is in his or her 'knower,' doubting decreases and belief grows to knowledge.

At the knowledge level, people often think that they heard wrong and need a new message from God, when something they were hoping for doesn't come to pass. Being fully persuaded is when the Word of God in your heart is truth, and nothing anyone says can deter you.

Commitment comes when there are great shakings, and it seems all is lost, but you stand in peace and know that God is on the throne. This was exemplified when Paul and Silas were on the boat in a storm. They knew their God.

How do we become fully persuaded? By believing that the Word of God is truth and everything else is a lie. Also, praying the Word of God over our circumstances, "knowing in your knower," and resisting doubt and fear.

In Hebrews 3:14 it says, "We are made partakers of Christ, if we hold the beginning of our confidence steadfast unto the end" (KJV). God would say to you in your time of challenge and testing, "Be still and know THAT I AM GOD" (Psalm 46:10, NIV).

Praying About Job Change

One of His disciples said to Him, "Lord, teach us to pray…"

Luke 11:1

Prayer actually changes me more than it changes my circumstances. Most people come to God when all else fails or they are at their wits' end. I call them "crisis Christians."

Sometimes my children are very self sufficient, doing their own thing, going their own way, until they get in trouble. Then they call mom or dad for help or prayer.

That is how many baby Christians relate to their Father God. We bring our problems and needs to God, but God wants us to bring ourselves to Him on a regular basis, praying about all things at all times, so that He can direct us and keep the problems from occurring.

He truly does want to protect us from Satan's traps, and He wants to prevent us from falling. Our self-sufficiency keeps us away from God until we think we need Him.

God is more interested in working miracles in our inner nature than He is in working miracles in our external circumstances. Nowhere is the question of "prayer changing me" versus "prayer changing things" more critical than in the marketplace.

So many people I talk to are unhappy in their jobs. Sometimes God allows "needles in the nest" to cause us to take flight into new opportunities.

Other times, God wants us to grow in the midst of our circumstances. Only prayer and time with God can help us know what to do.

John Maxwell, in his book *Life @ Work,* asks the question, "Is my current career moving me toward my skill set or away from it? Maxwell reminds us that work life will not be easy with any job we take anywhere, but it is okay to evaluate if the actual job we have matches the kind of work we have been called to do.

"If I hold a job doing work I am good at, in an organization that is sub-par, the situation is quite different from when I am being asked to do work that I am not equipped to handle" (Maxwell). Maxwell gives the example of Daniel being a good administrator for multiple kings over his lifetime, but for the most part, the kings themselves were despots.

"This was not a fun job. God called him to work in that less-than-perfect context, yet fully prepared him to do his work with excellence" (Maxwell).

Having "fun" may not be the criteria for being in the right place. Benjamin Franklin said, "All human situations have their inconveniences. We feel the inconveniences of the present, but neither see nor feel those of the future; and hence we often make troublesome changes without amendment, and frequently for the worse."

Maxwell writes, "Ask yourself, is the tension I feel just the natural pain of God growing me in my work, or is it a symptom of a bad fit? Sometimes it is time for a job change, but sometimes I am the one who needs to be changed."

Maxwell, who spoke at the Leadership Summit 2005, also states that even if God is stretching you in your current job position or asking you to jump into a new job opportunity, He will ALWAYS use the gifts He gave you and not ask you to do something you are not qualified to do.

Are you at your wits' end? Then come to your Creator who designed you for a purpose while you were in your mother's womb, and ask Him to either change things to align with that purpose, or change you to accept things as part of your purpose. I think, in our hearts, we already know the answer.

The War Room

When you pray, go into your room, and when you have shut your door, pray to your Father who is in the secret place; and your Father who sees in secret will reward you openly.

Matthew 6:6 NKJV

Do you battle with wandering thoughts in your mind when you come to God in prayer? I do. I try to focus, and before I know it my wheels are spinning planning out the day.

I find the best thing to do is to start praying for others. The Holy Spirit quickly enters into selfless prayers, and soon I begin to sense things in my spirit that I need to turn over to God.

Spending time in the prayer room helps us make decisions in the marketplace. There are several powerful stories of Christian CEO's in a book by Larry Julian titled *God Is My CEO: Following God's Principles in a Bottom-Line World.*

There were two CEO's depending on God and prayer to lead them through a tough decision. Through prayer, God gave each one the patience he needed.

One received patience to persevere and not let go of his plan; the other received patience to let go of his desire to climb the corporate ladder. For both, prayer was the practical tool they used to make the decision about God's will for their lives.

The most powerful prayers are the ones that confirm His promises in the Word and thank Him for His answers.

I have also learned that when you are in the prayer closet, and your mind wanders, write down the things that come to the surface, and give them to God as you write them. You will be surprised how a couple of those responsibilities or people were what or whom God wanted you to pray for in the first place.

Letting those thoughts come and writing them down, clears the way for the more focused prayer.

Soar Like an Eagle

Blessed are the poor in spirit…

Matthew 5:3

"Poor in spirit" means admitting that we are unable to do the task. When we admit that we cannot, that is when God rejoices, because He gets it done through us.

It is in those moments we proclaim, "I can do all things through Christ which {strengthens} me" (Philippians 4:13, KJV). An evangelist/pastor once said to me, "You feel totally empty right now after two years of doing nothing. Great! Now God can fill you with Himself because there is nothing of you left!"

That was good news, because at the time I had no skill or education for what He was calling me to do. When we believe we are poor in our ability to succeed, that is when Jesus Christ accomplishes His work through us.

When I meditate on what the possibilities are for the next level of leadership, I truly feel inadequate and unprepared for the task. Yet, going into the unknown or a new level of skill and growth is usually God's will for our lives.

When we feel poor in the spirit in our waiting season, we can be assured that when it is His time, He will fill us with Himself, and we will be able to give Him all the glory. In the end, it will be all about Him, not about us.

I once heard a story about a baby eagle raised by a farmer along with his chickens. When it came time for the eagle to soar, he thought he was a chicken and would not fly.

When tossed from the top of the barn by the farmer, he would return to the earth to enjoy eating the chicken feed with his peers. The farmer finally took him to a mountaintop and tossed him in the air, and he soared.

Are you waiting on God for His purpose in your life? He may have to toss you from a mountaintop so you will soar.

Waiting Versus Walking

But those who wait on the Lord... shall walk and not faint.
Isaiah 40:31 NKJV

Since I love variety and change, I believe that walking is better than waiting. However, the greatest growth in my life came through waiting upon God not moving forward in my own strength and timing.

When we wait, we are actually keeping the Lord before us, keeping our eyes on Him, and staying "tuned" to the next direction. Waiting keeps us from getting ahead of the Lord and allows for His perfect timing and His highest will to be accomplished in our lives and in others.

In waiting we learn to understand the reality of God's presence, not just the awareness of it. We learn to trust Him based on His Word, not on our experiences.

Everyone's waiting experiences are different. Some wait to conceive a child; others wait for a new job opportunity; and others wait for a healing from loss, rejection, or grief.

Without the growth of waiting, how would we ever get to a state of mind and heart where "we will not fear, though the earth be removed, and though the mountains be carried into the midst of the sea; though the waters thereof roar and be troubled, though the mountains shake?" (Psalm 46:2-3, KJV).

The wilderness experiences test our trust in God and cause us to wait upon Him. If we abide in Him, walk before Him (listening carefully), and trust the reality of His presence in our lives, we can make everyday decisions with confidence.

In 1984, God led me to wait before Him in His Word for 18 months until He gave me the next direction for my life. Toward the end of the phase, I confessed to a friend that I felt useless and that I was doing nothing for the kingdom of God or for my life.

She told me that the "waiting" was so powerful that the enemy wanted to discourage me and stop it because the strength and wisdom of the Lord was going down deep in my spirit. I proceeded to continue to wait with a little more interest in the process.

A short time later, I was called to run for school board and to a nationwide traveling/lobbying ministry. The stories of leaders in the Bible and the messages of Psalm and Proverbs became the sword and shield I needed to survive, and in my waiting, I suddenly turned into an eagle in full flight carried by the winds of God.

What is the difference between the eagle and other birds? They all fly, but the eagle soars.

"But they that wait upon the Lord shall renew their strength; they shall mount up with wings as eagles; they shall run, and not be weary; they shall walk, and not faint" (Isaiah 40: 31, KJV).

Secret Plans

...I did not immediately confer with flesh and blood

Galatians 1:16

There are times when we are to seek the counsel of other Christians, and times when we need to remain silent and rely on God's direction. I learned years ago that we only receive from God as much responsibility and information as we are willing to keep quiet about.

What that means is that God has plans for us, and He begins to stir those plans in our hearts. Instead of meditating and praying on it, we begin broadcasting to others what God is telling us, even when He was expecting us to keep it a secret.

This not only opens the door to doubt and skepticism against God's ideas, there is also the strong possibility you have just spoiled the timing of God's plan and "let the cat out of the bag" before He was ready. More than likely, people will not catch your vision, and they will discourage you and cause you to give up.

Apostle Paul was told by God to preach salvation to the Gentiles – something extremely controversial for a converted Jew. Paul said, "I did not confer with flesh and blood (did not consult or counsel with any frail human being or communicate with anyone). Nor did I (even) go up to Jerusalem to those who were Apostles (special messengers of Christ) before I was, but I went away and retired into Arabia" (Galatians 1:16-17).

Paul followed the dictates of God, not the criticisms of men. If God calls you to a great task, I can guarantee that others will not understand the step you are taking.

God has called my husband and me to many unusual decisions in our service to Him, and we have learned to only share with a select few before we step forward into the plan. When we do step out, we are already confident in our decision before God, because we have decided to serve God, not men.

Has God placed something in your heart? Let it simmer there for a while, and spend time in prayer about it. Let Him bring to you additional information and confirmation. Allow Him to build a confidence in you and prepare you.

God may not give you all the details, but He will give you Himself and give you the assurance and courage to step out in faith.

Every Phase of Our Life

…that I may know Him…

Philippians 3:10 NASB

Is the Lord with us even in the smallest details of our lives? The fact that He washed the disciples' feet tells me that Jesus is part of even the most humble tasks we perform.

I think we have more energy and focus at work when we have a new and exciting project to work on. When we are responsible for repetitive tasks that seem meaningless, it is more difficult for us to see God's purpose in our lives.

In 2005, I heard two of my friends talk about their experiences regarding a mission trip to Nicaragua where they worked on building an orphanage. One said that it was a good trip, but that she was expecting to do something more significant and impacting in people's lives The other said that she wished she could have worked on the construction rather than teach the children.

They both came to the humble conclusion that God was telling them, "It's not about you and your feelings – it's about doing what I, the Lord, need you to do and ministering even in the smallest, most insignificant way." They both came to realize they were indeed doing the work of the Lord.

As an educator, I get several weeks off in the summer. The hours I get to read inspirational books, study the Word, write Bible studies, fellowship, travel, and pray is like being on a mountaintop.

The thought of returning to the daily grind and responsibility of work can be a challenge. Through this Scripture in Philippians, I know that He will be with me in the mundane as well as the dynamic phases of my life, and that it is God's will for us to come down from the mountaintop, go into the valley, and minister for Him.

If I keep my eyes on Jesus and do not allow the enemy to distract me with my own expectations instead of God's, I will see the opportunities He has for me in service to others. It is my desire to know Jesus even in the small details of my life.

The Dream Buster

We do not have a High Priest who cannot sympathize with our weaknesses,
but One who has been tempted in all things as we are, yet without sin.

Hebrews 4:15 NASB

When we accept Jesus in our heart, we then come to understand His temptation to be enticed away from God's will. Just doing bad things does not assist Satan in his plan to destroy the work of God. However, when we succumb to temptation and think God could never use us, this is what keeps us from doing the things God intended us to do.

As soon as Jesus accepted His mission at His baptism, He was led into the wilderness where He was tested by the devil to give up His mission. He came out of the wilderness spiritually intact, not weary or exhausted, and not having shifted His point of view to believe something other than what God told Him.

The devil keeps us exhausted, discouraged, and guilty with the temptations of the flesh, when all along it is nothing but a distraction to keep us from achieving our mission. Be determined in your heart right now to pick up that dream God gave you, to press forward with that vision you once had, and to believe once again that you were created for a special purpose and a plan.

Do not leave this earth without fulfilling the call God has on your life. Do not be tempted to give up and to shift your point of view to believe "there never was a plan" or "it is now too late."

Jesus can sympathize with your weakness, with your weariness, and with your doubts and fears. He experienced all of those things in the wilderness and overcame them. Call upon Him, and He will help you.

Know that it is never too late, and God can redeem the time. Also remember, that the wilderness experience of temptation is used of God to prepare us.

It was the Holy Spirit that led Jesus into the wilderness. "Count it all joy when you fall into various trials, knowing that the testing of your faith produces patience. But let patience have its perfect work, that you may be perfect and complete, lacking nothing" (James 1: 2-4, NKJV).

Bruce Wilkinson, author of *The Dream Giver,* calls doubts and fears "dream busters" and writes, "So refuse to buy into the lie that your 'Waste Land' is too hard. It's not too hard. It's not too long. Your tests in the desert are the best answer to one of your deepest desires and prayers: 'Please make me into the person I need to be to do the dream You have created me for!'"

God gave me a "point of view" very early in my walk with Him, that I was called to be a leader. Many temptations in the form of doubt, fear, failure, persecution and personal trials have tried to stop that plan.

In the end, all of these trials made me into the leader I am today and will continue to make me into the leader He is creating for tomorrow. Before David, the shepherd and Goliath-killer, became King, he learned through a long pruning season how to submit to authority, lead men, endure, and trust God in trying circumstances.

Through it all, God gave him strength, productivity, and spiritual power to complete the dream God had for him. "For you, O God, have proved us; You have tried us as silver is tried, refined, and purified… (to abundance and refreshment and the open air" (Psalm 66:10-12).

Keep your point of view focused on Him and on the dream, and beware of the "dream buster."

The Danger of Tradition

Where is the wise man (the philosopher)? Where is the scribe (the scholar)? Where is the investigator (the logician, the debater) of this present time and age? Has not God shown up the nonsense and the folly of the world's wisdom?
1 Corinthians 1: 20

There are many Christian doctrinal traditions that hinder the work of the Lord. Throughout my entire Christian walk I have been pressured by the external voices of people who view the world through the filters of their own experience, tradition, or doctrine.

With God's calling on my life as a woman in leadership, I have had to carefully listen to my Lord's voice, and not the voice of well-meaning people. Here are some examples of God giving me direction, and Christians viewing it through their filters:

I opened four Christian pre-school/day care centers and one public school day care under God's leading. Christians in the 1970's told me that I was making it easy for women to go to work and that I was destroying the family through my efforts. Today, it is not even a concern among God's people.

With God's confirmation, we put our children in public school instead of private Christian school. Several Christians "warned us" that God did not want our children in public school. Today, the same believers realize you cannot protect your children forever and have come to understand the importance of being the salt and light in public schools.

I ran for school board because of clear direction and confirmation from God. Two pastors said they could not support me because women should not be in a political leadership position, and also because the Christian church should not be in politics. Since then, there has been a Christian grassroots movement in politics with both men and women involved.

I went to work for the phone company (together with my husband) as a telephone installer. My pastor and sisters-in-the-Lord at the time said that I was taking a job away from a man that needed to provide for his family. Today, almost all women are in the workforce and many in non-traditional jobs. People do not even mention this concern anymore.

In all these situations, God had a specific plan for my life. Do you see how dangerous these traditional points of view and judgments could be?

We need to be careful not to be a "dream buster" in someone's life, causing doubt and fear against what the Lord has directed him or her to do. When we give advice to people, it needs to be wisdom and knowledge from the Lord, not our own opinions based on our own tradition, or we may be in danger of stopping the mighty work of our Lord.

God's ways are not our ways. When you wait on God for direction, He will give you the strength to do what He calls you to do and the wisdom and courage to overcome the voices of opposition.

God's Purpose for Your Life

And I will give you the treasurers of darkness and hidden riches of secret places, that you may know that it is I, the Lord, the God of Israel, Who calls you by your name.

Isaiah 45:3

Did you know that God's purpose for your life is not impacted by your circumstances? Your circumstances mean nothing to what He has planned for you.

God's promises for you are not altered one bit by the fact that you may have spent half your life in sin; that you married too young; or that you got saved late in life. There is absolutely nothing that God cannot handle and absolutely nothing that can stop the hand of God.

When you think about God's calling on your life, do not let the term "missionary" deter you from receiving God's direction. We are all missionaries wherever we serve, called to be examples for Christ.

As the world gets darker and the pressures get greater, people are watching the strength, peace, and joy that rest upon us. At some point, like moths, they will be drawn to that light, because they desperately need it.

The Bible is not a textbook of doctrine – it is a textbook of people's stories and lives. It is a book of stories of men and women who walked with God. It's about character and wisdom. You have a story too – but it will not be written in the Book of Life unless you start living your story to the fullest.

What is the real point of our existence? Jesus boiled it all down to two things: loving God and loving others. Do this, He said, and you will find the purpose of your life.

Everything else will fall into place. Find what your talent is and give it to the world. Because of your love toward God, you have a special assignment to give God's love to others. Everything you need is in your heart.

Rick Warren in his book *The Purpose Driven Life* has taught thousands of Christians that there are five basic purposes for our life:

> You were planned for God's pleasure (develop a friendship with God)

> You were formed for God's family (find a place to belong and restore broken fellowship)

> You were created to become like Christ (continue to grow in your faith, overcoming temptation)

> You were shaped for serving God (accept the assignment He has given you)

> You were made for a mission.

> What is your mission? Your mission is simply sharing your life message, living a life for Christ, keeping your life in balance, and living with a purpose.

The next time you see the word "missionary," don't think about China and Africa (unless God is calling you there) – think about the marketplace you are in right now, and let God's strength, peace, love, and joy flow out to others right where you are.

Boil It Down

For I know the thoughts and plans that I have for you, says the Lord, thoughts and plans for welfare and peace and not for evil, to give you hope in your final outcome.

Jeremiah 29: 11

Are you trying to find purpose and direction? Sometimes we make seeking our purpose in life too complex.

Jesus used to boil it all down into simple phrases like, "he who has lost his life for My sake will find it" (Matthew 10:39, NKJV). He also said that the laws (or we could say our life) boil down to this one thing – "Love the Lord your God with all your heart and with all your soul, and with all your mind...and love your neighbor as yourself" (Matthew 22:36, 39, NIV)

Laurie Beth Jones, points out: "if we understand our core values, we could save years of doubt, confusion, and misplaced energy as we try to find direction for our life." But Jesus boiled it down best when He said, "If you want to be happy, do these things."

NIKE boiled it down to "Just Do It," and it became an award winning campaign. Everything the United States stands for can be boiled down to one word: freedom.

Just ask yourself, if you had to boil down your message or gift to the world, what would it be? Discover what your gift is, and use it.

Jesus said in Matthew 25:29, "To those who use well what they are given, even more will be given, and they will have an abundance. But from those who do nothing, even what little they have will be taken away" (NLT). In other words, use it or lose it.

Jesus is our best example of giving His talent. As Laurie Beth Jones points out, Jesus said, "Yes, I will come to your party. Yes, I will meet your mother-in-law. Yes, I will heal your daughter. Yes, I will do what you ask of me."

Jesus boiled it down to one word - "yes."

Silence is Golden

(Even) when He heard that Lazarus was sick, He still stayed two days longer in the same place where He was.

John 11:6

Jesus waited in Bethany for two days AFTER He heard that Lazarus was dying. Lazarus was a good friend of Jesus, yet Jesus did not rush to his side. He WAITED on God's direction.

This is a great example of the Lord taking all his directions from His Father and not coming under the pressure of His friends, or His enemies, who probably accused Him of having no compassion.

Jesus knew that when doing God's work, timing is everything. The Spirit had told Him that the situation was "not unto death, but for the glory of God" (John 11:4, KJV). If Jesus had gotten ahead of the Lord, the miracle of raising Lazarus from the dead may have never taken place.

Often in the waiting time, there is also silence. It is in the silent times that God is bringing you into His deeper purposes. It is in the WAIT times that we renew our strength because we are about to soar like eagles.

In November 1998, I had completed two degrees and worked for three companies over a three-year period learning multiple skills – all part of God's direction and plan. I suddenly found myself at the end of the road with no direction. I wrote in my journal:

> *"There is such a stillness in my life. It is the end of the road of all the milestones God required of me. Now I don't even know why I did it. I have walked in the ordinary of the workplace for so long, I am now content to be ordinary. I am so used to being empty, I don't care if I am ever full again. I don't know who I am or what God's plan is. I'm very tired and I just need to rest. At least I know that when I am empty – He can fill me with Himself. I also know He can be a God of "suddenlies" and everything can change in a moment."*

Since I had no clear direction, I decided to rest and not worry about the future and spend time in prayer, trusting Him in the silence.

Ecclesiastes 3:1-7 says: "To everything there is a season, and a time for every matter or purpose under heaven …A time to get and a time to lose, a time to keep and a time to cast away…a time to keep silent and a time to speak."

In that time of silence, I said "no" to many opportunities that were from man (world and church) and not from God. I waited in "my Bethany." Eight months later, God opened a door for a job in California and God said, "Go!" Suddenly I was moving from Washington State to Palm Springs, and God had a whole new adventure awaiting me.

Bloom Where You are Planted

I have become all things to all men so that by all possible means I might save some.

1 Corinthians 9:22

When considering the work assignments God has given you, here are some encouraging words to remind you that you are exactly where God wants you to be today. Consider the following:

God's viewpoint is TODAY. We take on life and work for Him "bit by bit" not worrying about the future.

God's viewpoint is that we are here for one purpose only – to put our lives in captivity to Jesus Christ, no matter what the difficulties.

We must not always ask God to take us somewhere else, but allow God to turn the ordinary into the extraordinary right where we are.

We have not chosen God, but He has chosen us, and we are here for His purpose "in His college," where He is molding us for His eternal purposes.

Let God have His way with you, and bloom where you are planted. If He wants to call you to something else, He will do it.

In a financial Bible study I participated in, I read several Scriptures that confirm that our employment is of God and meant to be part of our productive lives for Him. There is not one Scripture about retirement in the Bible.

Paul ran the race to the very end, working hard at making tents to pay his own way. If we are blessed with enough money to retire, then perhaps it is to pursue being a worker for God more fully in the church or missionary field. I heard a sermon that encouraged us to pray a "dangerous prayer," and give our lives completely over to God for HIS PURPOSE and ask Him to use us right where we are.

So often I dream of not having to work anymore, but I now see that this is only draining my energy to dream about something that may not be God's will. It is causing me to think of a "perfect future" instead of focusing on God's viewpoint for me today. My prayers need to daily be for God to give me the strength to do His will right where He has me by His design and to thank Him for molding me into the image of Jesus Christ so that others may come to Him through me.

A cab driver in San Antonio who grew up in Mexico understands this principle. He told me that he followed the simple beliefs of Jesus without the politics.

He said, "Jesus said to treat the rich and poor as equals. I do not see too much of that in America. So I try to do that – be kind to every passenger in my cab no matter who they are or how they behave. I think faith in God is that simple - I call it being part of the brotherhood of all mankind."

Now there is a man who knows how to bloom where he is planted.

A Compass for Our Life

And try to learn what is pleasing to the Lord;(let your lives be constant proofs of what is most acceptable to Him).

Ephesians 5:10

Our relationship with God and our knowledge of His will by reading the Word of God should be so strong that we would not have to ask for guidance in every detail of our life. If the peace of the Lord is with us, then we are on track. If we are walking in obedience, then we are headed in the right direction.

When a normally obedient child chooses to disobey, he or she suffers internal conflict. As children of God, we too receive signals in our inner being and learn to recognize what is not from God.

The Holy Spirit is a compass for our lives. That compass is what helps us make decisions without a lot of emotion or fanfare. We can sense when the needle is not heading "north" to God.

In the marketplace, decisions cannot be made without ethical consideration. John C. Maxwell wrote a book entitled, *There's No Such Thing as Business Ethics: There's Only One Rule for Making Decisions.* In other words – it is not complex – you simply do what is right. As an international presenter, he uses the *Golden Rule* to teach ethics in business, because it crosses all cultures and all religions.

We need to manage others and ethically do business with others the way we want to be managed and the way we want other businesses to ethically deal with us. Maxwell and other Christian leaders believe, "if we get that one rule right, no other rules are needed."

Ted Koppel, former newscaster, said, "There's harmony and inner peace to be found in following a moral compass that points in the same direction regardless of fashion or trend."

I once asked a Christian advisor, "Do you think some of these trials in my life are because God is putting needles in the nest so I will take flight to somewhere else?"

I loved His answer. "I do not know of any Scripture that says 'God has to make you miserable so you can get direction from Him.' God will more than likely reveal to you what you need to do, and if there is a change, He will simply open a door and ask you to step through."

I was once again reminded that my every day circumstances are by God's design, and if there is a new direction, God will change the design, not me. If I am being faithful and my compass is on course, then I can be at peace and not have to ask a lot of questions.

Are you lacking peace or confused about the direction you are heading? Then stop, pray, change course and get the needle back on north. Let the Lord restore your sense of direction.

Bungee Jumping with Jesus

"He went out, not knowing where he was going."

Hebrews 11:8 NASB

The book of Hebrews offers a review of great people of faith in the Old Testament. Abraham was asked to pull up his tent stakes and go to an unknown place where he would receive his inheritance.

Renowned public speaker and leader, John Maxwell says that these men and women had the vision to see an invisible future. Their assurance of God's promises gave them vision for tomorrow. In *The Maxwell Leadership Bible,* he writes, "their dreams, not their memories, consumed them."

The Holy Spirit is reminding me that I can be so busy seeking the Christian walk or seeking my destiny, I forget to seek the source – Jesus. Going all out is when we completely trust the one who is leading us.

Jesus is a pretty radical guy to follow. As I take another "walk" through the four Gospels, I am discovering a rebel – not a behind the scenes religious man. He touched the leper (something forbidden), called the religious leaders "snakes", discussed religion with a woman, healed on the Sabbath in defiance to the Pharisees, boldly proclaimed the good news when told to stop, and called himself King in a kingdom where Caesar was "god."

In light of all this, I truly have to search my soul and ask, "Will I go all out to do whatever this Son of God calls me to do? Will I abandon self, or worry about what others think?"

Everyone is caught up in "reality television shows," yet we are avoiding the larger than life reality of the Lord's call to lay down our lives for Him. The true reality show is going to be the one we watch in heaven on how we lived our lives for Jesus.

Years ago, my brother and I did a duo-swing bungee ride at a county fair. We were catapulted into the air, left to the bounce and spin of a crazy ride, wondering if we would return to earth safely.

In my mind, I have a radical picture of bungee jumping with Jesus. I can visualize the freefall, but I also see Him hanging on to me and not letting go.

Perhaps you are not yet in the dream or vision you expected at this stage of your life because you are not yet ready to be radical – to abandon all. Consider letting go of earthly things that do not matter, and jumping with Jesus. My prayer for you (and me) is to relax, trust Him, and enjoy the ride.

Called

I heard the voice of the Lord, saying, "Whom shall I send? And who will go for Us?" Then I said, "Here am I; send me."

Isaiah 6:8

"It's my calling" or "I've been called" is not heard much in the secular world. Even among Christians, people see their pastor as "called," but not themselves. There is a misunderstanding about the world "called" or "calling."

In this passage of Scripture, the Lord did not call Isaiah. Isaiah overheard the Lord talking and joyfully responded, "I'll go!"

Our first calling is to have a relationship with Jesus Christ and learn to know His voice. "Many are called, but few are chosen" (Matthew 22:14, NASB) is somewhat of a "mystery Scripture."

I liken it unto a vision that one of my spiritual teachers had. She saw two roads leading toward heaven. One was very narrow with very few people on it, and one was very wide and very crowded. They were all headed in the same direction, and they all believed in God. Occasionally one of the followers on the wide path would step over into the narrow path.

It struck me that the wide path seemed busy with lots of fellowship, but the narrow path seemed very lonely. God never forces us to respond to the call. He never says, "Get over in that path, I need you." He simply says to the people in the wide path, "I need you all because the harvest is great and the laborers are few, will you come?"

There are all walks of life and situations that God calls His people to – it is not just the mission field in Africa, church leadership, or working for a national Christian organization. He calls people to politics, to teaching, to executive leadership, or to move to a new company, or new location.

Mostly He calls us to minister to the hurting and needy people all around us and to pray for them. John Maxwell, author of *Life @ Work*, refers to the calling on General William Booth who started the Salvation Army. Booth shared, "While women weep, as they do now, I'll fight; while children go hungry, as they do now, I'll fight; while men go to prison, in and out, in and out, as they do now, I'll fight; while there is a drunkard left, while there is a poor lost girl upon the streets, while there remains one dark soul without the light of God, I'll fight – I'll fight to the very end!"

Maxwell asks, "Are you fighting for the individuals where you work (or in your neighborhood), or do you just pass them by in the hall (or on the street)?" He reminds us that people all around us are stripped of their self-confidence, self-worth, hope, faith, purity, meaning, and opportunity. They are abandoned, lonely, gripped by fear and doubt. If we just get to know them, we will discover their hurt and need.

Your calling (or profession) may be as a teacher, but you are called to teach students character, integrity, and life skills. Your calling may be construction worker, but you are called to be an example of Jesus in the workplace. Your calling may be doctor or nurse, but you are called to show the love of God to your patients. Your calling may be manager, but you are called to coach and encourage employees in new skills and self-confidence.

We can live our lives just performing our calling, or we can hear the call of Jesus who said, "If you love me, feed my sheep," and begin to be sensitive to the needs around us.

The Call of God

No eye has seen, no ear has heard, no mind has conceived what God has prepared for those who love Him.

1 Corinthians 2:9 NIV

Most Christians think that a "call of God" means being called to be a pastor or called to the mission field. The truth is, most of us are called to serve in the marketplace (workplace), neighborhood, and our local church in some capacity. Our service and our jobs are an overflow of who we are and the gifts that God gave us.

Shortly after I received Jesus as my Savior, I read the book *The Cross and the Switchblade.* In this story, Pastor David Wilkerson went to the streets of New York and delivered Nicky Cruz from a gang. Nicky became a great evangelist for youth.

I had two small children at the time, and I recall weeping and crying out to God, "Oh Lord, it's too late for me. If I had met you before I married and had children, I could have served you on the streets of New York! If there is anything you can use me for as a wife and mother, please show me what it is."

Within the hour (really!!) the telephone rang and the Christian education director from our church called and asked if I would coordinate the nursery-scheduling ministry. I was silent for a moment, and then remembered my prayer, and said, "Yes."

This small step of obedience eventually led to Sunday school teacher of pre-school children to middle-school children, founder and director of two church pre-school daycare centers, church Christian education director, local school board member, education lobbyist, president of the American Parents Association, and finally professor in education. My service and obedience unto the Lord revealed the call of God on my life.

Demos Shakarian wrote the book *The Happiest People on Earth.* His message was simple: "Find out what your gifts are and use them and you will be happy. Do not try to do something that does not come natural to you and you will become one of the happiest people on earth doing what you love to do."

What is interesting about the things God called me to is that I did not even know at the time that I would love doing them. A close relationship with God will reveal to you what your "natural call" is.

There are many tools to help evaluate what your gifts are. Take the time to discover the unique person God created and ask Him how HE wants to use those gifts for the kingdom of God here on earth.

A Rein-Trained Horse

I (the Lord) will instruct you and teach you in the way you should go; I will counsel you with My eye upon you. Be not like the horse or the mule, which lack understanding, which must have their mouths held firm with bit and bridle, or else they will not come with you.

Psalm 32: 8 -9

This message is short, powerful, and to the point. There was a time in my Christian walk when I would get direction or a vision, then grow impatient with the fulfillment. I would either try to make it happen or fill my life with busy activities to "fill in the blanks" of nothingness.

A friend called and said, "The Lord gave me a vision of a stubborn horse, and He wants you to quit kicking against His will or running off without his lead. You need to rein-in with your Master."

Later, we researched and found the Scripture verses of Psalm 32: 8-9 (above). I had attended horse camp as a child and teenager, and I knew the Lord wanted me to yield and be as responsive as a rein-trained horse. Rein-trained horses only need the small pressure of the reins on the neck to move in the direction of his or her master.

It took courage for my friend to give me that vision, but it changed the course of my life and prevented a great deal of unnecessary grief and torment. God knows everything about everything, and if we yield to Him in our times of darkness and waiting, He will lead us. Just be still, wait, and listen.

May His Force Be With You

Roll your works upon the Lord (commit and trust them wholly to Him; He will cause your thoughts to become agreeable to His will, and) so shall your plans be established and succeed.

Proverbs 16:3

Apostle Paul describes his calling as a necessity laid upon him. That means no matter what his mind tells him or how his heart tries to discourage him, something in his spirit drove him to be an evangelist until the day he died.

Some people are afraid of receiving "a call" from God, because they think it will be so big, so difficult, or so time consuming, they will not be able to do it. I can attest that it is not like that.

When God drops a call into your spirit to do something, it is like a "force" that drives you and consumes you and you have a desire to do it. In fact, you are miserable if you don't do it.

I served as the faculty advisor to "Student Christian Club" at the college I worked at. Each year it was a challenge to get the district to agree to a room location, to provide audiovisual equipment for educational videos, or to coordinate non work-related activities in my work schedule. It was God's call, so I let God work it out.

Each semester a room would open up, and God would give me the time and leaders to help. Through the club, at least two students accepted Jesus as their Savior, and each year, dozens of Christian students were encouraged through Biblical teachings. Toward the end of my service, pastors were volunteering from all over the community from different denominations to meet the students and share a message of faith.

If you do not feel called to your job, or if you do not have a clear sense of God's purpose for your life, begin to pray for that direction immediately. Spend time in prayer, discover what your gifts and talents are (those things you love to do), be open to God using you right where you are, and journal your thoughts and ideas to help you explore what God created you for in this world.

Part 3
Overcoming Challenges

Always and Never

If we (freely) admit that we have sinned and confess our sins, He is faithful and just (true to His own nature and promises) and will forgive our sins and (continuously) cleanse us from all unrighteousness.

1 John 1:9

I have learned that the path of sin usually starts with some thoughts in our mind placed there by the enemy. It can be thoughts of jealousy, resentment, anger, hopelessness, doubt, criticism, or fear.

Two of the most powerful words the devil uses to discourage us are "always" and "never." These two words come against the promises of God.

The enemy will tell you the situation has always been like this, and it will never change. We begin to panic and the next thought is, "If that is true, then I better fix it myself."

The lies of the enemy will trick us into making decisions that are not in conformity with God's will and purpose. Many people divorce because their thought processes tell them, "If I stay married, I will never reach my dreams and goals, or I will always be unhappy."

We need to submit our thoughts to the Lord before they become actions of sin. Jesus teaches us that thoughts of hate lead to murder, and thoughts of lust lead to adultery. He warns that we will be judged for our thoughts, not just our actions.

The good news is, that because of what Jesus did on the cross, and because of the blood He shed for both our thoughts and actions, our confession defeats the lies of Satan and brings us into fellowship with God. Do not let the enemy lie to you and tell you that you will always fail or you will never get it right.

The Bible says, "And let us not lose heart and grow weary and faint in acting nobly and doing right, for in due time and at the appointed season we shall reap, if we do not loosen and relax our courage and faint" (Galatians 6:9).

God is on your side! Fight the good fight! Do not let the enemy keep you from sweet fellowship with our Lord.

Peace in the Storm

Peace I leave with you, My peace I give to you ... "
                                    John 14: 27 NASB

Have you been through some storms in your life, or are you in the middle of one right now? Perhaps you have lived long enough to know that there will more than likely be another storm down the road and still waters do not last forever. Think back for a moment on a storm you went through, whether recently or long ago.

Did it feel like the ship was going to sink? Were you a little seasick – full of anxiety - from the crashing waves? Perhaps it was the final outcome that made it so frightening.

In a storm it is difficult to breathe, carry on with your life, and there is a constant state of wondering if you will ever be normal again. We cannot stop the storms of life.

Jesus himself said, "In the world, ye shall have tribulation: but be of good cheer; I have overcome the world" (John 16:33). God wants you to be an overcomer. He wants you to keep your faith and to trust Him in the midst of your circumstances.

In the summer of 2005, I went through a small storm that reminded me of all the anxiety and challenge it takes to rest in God and keep the faith. Upon arrival at Washington, DC's Reagan National Airport, I left my wallet under the seat of the airplane by accident and didn't realize it until I got to the hotel.

In the wallet was $200 I had saved for meals and miscellaneous expenses, all my credit cards, my driver's license, faculty ID card (which was my only other picture ID) and social security card. Basically, I lost everything someone needs to steal my identity.

My daughter and I were fighting back the tears as we spent the first three hours of our vacation trying to resolve all the issues, from contacting credit card companies, United Airlines, and Homeland Security to figure out how I would get home in high alert without any identification. With prayer and doing everything possible, I still could not be at peace, and I could not sleep that night.

I was in spiritual warfare for my faith in God as I imagined all the worse case scenarios. I called my husband late at night, worried and disheartened, and he said, "It's in the Lord's hands now. You need to trust Him."

The words gave me peace, but over the next two days the anxiety and fear kept coming back. I cried out to God and said, "I am believing for a miracle. God help my unbelief."

I began to praise God and rejoice at how this was all going to be for His glory, and I sang to Him in that hotel room, entering His Rest. God overwhelmed me with peace, and my confidence was finally in Him, not in the circumstances.

I did not get my wallet back, but God protected my identity, restored my $200 in another way, and miraculously, I returned home on the flight with no identification. Most important, I had peace during the rest of my trip and enjoyed my vacation.

John 14:27 says, "Let not your heart be troubled" and Philippians 4: 6-7 says, "Do not fret or have any anxiety about anything, but in every circumstance and in everything, by prayer and petition (definite requests), with thanksgiving, continue to make your wants known to God. And God's peace (shall be yours, that tranquil state of a soul assured of its salvation through Christ, and so fearing nothing from God and being content with its earthly lot of whatever sort that is, that peace) which transcends all understanding shall garrison and mount guard over your hearts and minds in Christ Jesus."

May you receive His peace today – even *before* God solves the problem.

Spiritual Muscles

In the world ye shall have tribulation: but be of good cheer; I have overcome the world.

John 16: 33 KJV

When I moved to Palm Desert to take my present job at the college, I had to come eighteen months ahead of my husband while we waited for his retirement.

My job started on August 10, 1999. On August 2, 1999, before I drove from Washington to California, I have the following recorded in my journal as a question to the Lord: "Why does it have to be so hard? Other families relocate together. The last mission you called me on in Washington, D.C. we were separated then, too. Why do we have to be separated again? Are you sure we are doing the right thing?"

I read in my journal from the Washington, D.C. challenge, "God does not help us overcome life, He gives us life as we overcome. In our strain is actually our strength."

I began to laugh and cry at the same time and wrote in my journal a second time: "Of course this move is a strain! Of course this is ludicrously impossible for me! Because you want me to ludicrously depend on you! You want me to know you even more! You want to show me how You are my provider and how You are going to take care of every detail, give me favor, and give me strength."

I realized in that moment that God was once again stretching me because He wanted me to once again completely depend on Him.

During this time of preparation to move, I called my daughter who lived in Texas and shared with her how I was getting the strength to leave for my new job in a few days. I said to her, "I wonder what would have happened if I said 'no' when God asked me to run for school board? I wonder where I would be today if I said 'no' to living in Washington, D.C.? I wonder what would have happened if I said 'no' regarding getting my education? If I said 'no' to all those things, I would not be facing this decision right now."

My daughter replied, "Mommy" – she still called me Mommy – "I wouldn't be who I am today if you said 'no' to God. Because of the example you set, I had the courage to go to college and trust God to pay for it. I had the courage to leave home and come to Texas to teach. Look at all the good things that are happening to me in Texas. I'm growing in my Spanish language; I have a good job, and I met my husband. You influenced me so much, and my life is so much better because you said 'yes' to God."

God richly blessed me with those words. Every time I face new stretches and stresses, the timing brings me back to this devotion and these words of encouragement.

An evangelist once said, "Without pressure and resistance, we cannot build spiritual muscles." When messages like this start duplicating, I sense that many Christians are also dealing with great pressures.

I can assure you from experience, that the pressure is not forever, and when you get to the other side of these circumstances, you will have developed spiritual muscles for the next phase of your life.

Nothing Else Will Matter

In the year that King Uzziah died, I saw the Lord...
Isaiah 6:1 NIV

I am not sure if there is a significance to Isaiah's ministry as a prophet beginning the same year as King Uzziah's death in 740 B.C. Perhaps it is because there was a period of peace for the Israelites with this King, and Isaiah's gift of prophet was not yet needed.

After the king's death, the Assyrians conquered the land and introduced idolatry into the Jerusalem temple. The kings who followed did not welcome Isaiah's strong warnings, and eventually he was martyred by being sawed in half under Manasseh, the wicked son of Hezekiah.

Isaiah had a vision of the Lord, and the Lord was all he could see. He was willing to pay a price for that vision.

Isaiah had a tough responsibility to speak for approximately 80 years, delivering warnings to the wicked and promises of blessings to those who turned back to the Lord. What kept him going? His vision did not let him take anyone else into account, except God.

There was a season of preparation before Isaiah entered his full ministry. While we hope for the vision of God in our lives, we must spend our "waiting time" being accountable to God's teachings and allow His character-building process to take place in our lives.

God reveals truth to people of character. When God calls us, our character will be ready.

When Isaiah writes, "when you pass through the waters, I (the Lord) will be with you; and when you pass through the rivers, they will not sweep over you. When you walk through the fire, you will not be burned" (Isaiah 43:2, NIV). We can believe him knowing what he endured in his lifetime.

Some of the testing and trials we go through are because we know the promises of God and can share those promises with others. Many Christians, who read this devotion might think, "I could never answer the call of a Moses or Isaiah."

It has been my experience that when God calls you to a place that sets you apart from others, He will give you courage through His voice, vision, and words of knowledge through other Christians. It is the revelation of God that gives us the strength to endure.

That is why Joan of Arc is such an inspiration to me. At age fourteen, "the young maiden" led French troops into battle because she had a vision.

Whatever your calling is, He will prepare your character, He will equip you with everything you need, and He will not forsake you, even unto death. Once you see God the way Isaiah or Joan of Arc did, you will only want to do God's will, and nothing else will matter.

Dwelling in the Secret Place

Bringing every thought into captivity every thought to the obedience of Christ.

2 Corinthians 10:5 KJV

It is my heart's desire to invite God into my daily circumstances, but I often wait until circumstances are beyond my problem solving abilities to reach out for God's grace, mercy, and deliverance. Our analytical mind tells us that there is a time to abide in God and a time to abide in our work tasks.

What happens is that we delay spending time with God, hoping for a less stressful more peaceful moment when we can do some prayerful abiding. Jesus was totally peaceful in the middle of all his circumstances (feeding 5,000, false accusations, storms at sea, demon-possessed people, and even facing death) because He KNEW God's love, and He continually was abiding in his Father.

The same peace that Jesus had belongs to us, because He resides in our hearts. Jesus said, "abide in me and I will abide in you." It is the same formula He used with the Father.

We can walk our journey with the same serenity and trust in God that He had. The battle begins in our minds, and we must prevent fear, worry, stress, anger, or jealousy from getting into our spirits.

When the budget doesn't balance, the car breaks down, or the company starts laying people off, we need to bring those thoughts of fear and worry captive into the words of Christ, and we need to tell our spirit to be at peace. We need to trust that "God will supply all our needs according to His riches in glory" and "God will not forsake us."

We then invite God into the situation through prayer to help us problem solve. Close your eyes, breathe in His love, feel His presence just for a moment, and know the "peace of God, which surpasses all comprehension" (Philippians 4:7, NASB). Notice how you began to feel peace by just focusing on Him for a second?

Several people have written to me with concerns about job changes, life choices, unfair practices, and company downsizing. The circumstances in our life keep changing, but God does not change.

I encourage those in fear or anxiety to read Psalm 91. The first two verses talk about abiding: "He that {dwells} in the secret place of the most High shall abide under the shadow of the Almighty. I will say of the Lord, He is my refuge and my fortress: my God; in Him will I trust" (KJV).

There are at least a dozen promises in Psalm 91. Meditate on this list: God will protect you, deliver you, give His angels charge over you, defend you, preserve you, bear you up, feed you, provide for you, love you, honor you, cover you, keep evil from you, satisfy you, be faithful to you, and set you on high.

What do we have to do to receive all of that? Abide in Him – "because you have made the Lord your refuge, and the Most High your dwelling place."

Turning Fears Into Prayers

Casting the whole of your care (all your anxieties, all your worries, all your concerns, once and for all) on Him, for He cares for you affectionately, and cares about you watchfully.

1 Peter 5: 7

I have had several e-mails and phone calls this month from people who are frustrated with their lives, their jobs, or even with God. People need to vent, so I spent most of my time listening.

I heard the following comments: "I have prayed to God every morning for my need, why won't He answer my prayer?"

"My company is starting to downsize and my job is at risk, why is God doing this to me again, and why are those Hollywood actors wealthy when they don't even serve God?"

"I hate my job, but I sense that God is not going to move me on until I accept the situation. How do you know when He is allowing these circumstances, and when you should just quit?"

"I am trying so hard to be right with God, and I keep failing. When am I ever going to get it right?"

I observed that there was a 100% focus on the problem, on self, and a disbelief that God was in control. I say this not to judge, but to offer a solution.

"After Job had prayed for his friends, the LORD made him prosperous again and gave him twice as much as he had before" (Job 42:10, NIV). Jesus would say, "when you get your eyes off yourself and onto others, I will take care of your life." "Seek ye first the kingdom of God...and all these things shall be added unto you" (Matthew 6:33, KJV)

I have found that when I am focused on others in prayer, prayers regarding my life that I had forgotten about are suddenly answered. The disciples were only focused on the needs of others, yet all their needs were met – including paying taxes to Caesar while unemployed!

This is why Jesus said that God knows your needs BEFORE you even ask, and He will clothe you and feed you. If we trust God that ALL our needs are already taken care of, we can leave those things in His hands and spend our time praying for and ministering to others.

Do you need an answered prayer? Then start praying for someone else's prayer request.

Do you fear losing your job? Start praying for others in the organization, and pray for the welfare of the company and the management, not just yourself.

Do you hate your job? Ask God to show you why you are there and who you should be praying for.

Are you jealous of the wealth of others? Pray for their souls, and thank God for the gift of salvation and your inheritance in heaven.

Turn your frustrating "Job" experience into prayer for others without any expectation for your own life, and begin to experience God's peace and joy.

Remember, it was Satan who attacked Job. Perhaps if all of Satan's attacks turned into prayers for others, he would have to stop attacking. Now there is something to think about.

Old Faithful

The water that I will give him will become in him a well of water springing up to eternal life.

John 4:14 NASB

Jesus wants to be an overflowing fountain in our life. At our home in the desert, our lawn sprinkler system occasionally does not work, because some sand or a stone is blocking one of the sprinkler heads, and it has to be cleaned.

It is neither the fault of the water, nor the source of the water, but rather something is blocking the flow. Either our relationship is not right with the Lord, or it is not right with someone else.

In the first instance, you may be spending more time receiving than pouring out, and you are starting to dry up. If you do not share your blessings or your experiences with others, the flow will stop. In order to keep the river flowing, we are supposed to measure out into the lives of others with the same measure we receive.

In the second instance of obstruction, there could be anger, resentment or unforgiveness. Even if you do not feel like it, step out in faith and release that person who has hurt you. The situation is not worth blocking the flow and joy of God.

If you are staying close to your Source, Jesus, if you are pouring your life out to others, if you have no obstruction in your heart, and you do not see or feel the rivers of life pouring through you, there may be a quiet underground stream that will soon burst forth into a fountain. Sometimes the water sprinkler pops its own obstruction from built up water pressure. It bursts forth into a fountain pouring on everything within its reach.

Persistence in time of pressure is like that. Day after day we faithfully do what God requires of us, and then suddenly a light breaks forth at the end of the tunnel and our joy is full.

After ten years of attending school, studying the Word, working in high-pressured leadership positions and daily prayer, I was invited to speak at a women's retreat. It had been a long time since I had done church ministry.

Responding to the Lord's will, I prepared a message in the midst of my other responsibilities, including finishing my PhD. I poured my heart into the preparation and at the least expected a good teaching and possibly some prayer for a few women in need.

When I started teaching, the Holy Spirit showed up and rivers began to flow through me. The Lord was ministering healing, a word of encouragement and deliverance from fear or unforgiveness for multiple women.

At the end of three days, there was no one who was not blessed by the Lord. I was completely humbled and overwhelmed with God's presence.

For ten years the rivers were developing in my obedience, studies, and relationship with Him, and when I responded in obedience, it was a gushing river. If we are faithful, "Old Faithful" will show up!

Spiritual Confusion

Jesus replied, "You do not realize what you are asking."

Matthew 20:22

In this passage of Scripture, the mother of Zebedee's children asked Jesus if her two sons might sit at His right and left hand in the kingdom. Jesus replied, "Are you able to drink the cup that I am about to drink?"

He was asking, "Are you willing to go through a way that you temporarily do not understand? Are you willing to suffer spiritual confusion until you come to the understanding of what God wants for you?"

To go through a path of sorrow and suffering as Jesus did may not make spiritual sense, especially if it seems God is not responding to prayer. Jesus knew the outcome of his death, but others were spiritually confused.

In their minds, they probably thought that God had forsaken Him. Pastor and author Dr. David Jeremiah, says three things about God seeming indifferent to your situation: "1) When you think He does not hear, He is always near; 2) When you don't know what to do, remember WHO you know; and 3) When you cannot see God in your problems, you will see Him in your praise."

In 1975, God wanted me to take a job for two years with the phone company. My husband and I had strong direction from the Lord that it was His will. It absolutely did not make sense – but we allowed His will in my life.

It was one of the darkest times I ever experienced, and I can still feel the pain like it was yesterday. As a female telephone installer and pole climber, I was hated by most of the males on the crew.

I had gone from full-time Christian mom to this profession (I had received previous training in the military). Not only did I have to go to work every day and face extreme rejection and listen to immoral stories and language, I had to face a pastor and church friends who told me what I was doing was not of God. Because of their rejection, it felt like God had abandoned me.

I was so very much alone; yet I knew I was in God's perfect will. My relationship with the Father grew very close in those two years. While other crewmembers had lunch together, I sat in my truck and read the Bible.

When the two-year experience was over, I begged God to tell me why I went through the trial, but He was silent. Every year, I would ask at least once, "God, why did you have me work on such a hateful phone crew and allow the rejection of the church?" But He never answered.

In 1985, I was in the midst of a political and spiritual battle, running for school board, where literally thousands of people either loved me or hated me, because of the moral values I was standing for in my school district. Something negative was being written about me every single day in the local newspaper. I wanted to quit the race, but God had made it very clear to me and to my husband that this was His perfect will for our lives.

On election night, I won with 53% of the vote. I hurried home and collapsed with relief in my living room, but was weeping from the emotional exhaustion of so much rejection.

In that moment on the couch, ten years after I asked, God answered my question. I heard Him say in my spirit, "You worked on that phone crew to prepare for this moment in time. Without that previous suffering, you never would have made it." Are you confused? In time, God will make everything clear.

Trained for Battle

When you were under the fig tree, I saw you.

John 1:48 NKJV

In this passage of Scripture, Nathanael was relaxing under a fig tree. When things are going smooth, we tell ourselves that we are ready for the crisis – ready for the battle. But if we are not spending time in prayer and worship in the calm times, we will not be fit for battle, and our true character will be revealed.

Our relationship with God is essential for spiritual fitness and war-readiness. Our worship in our everyday occasions prepares and strengthens us. If you think you have no time for prayer or Bible study, not only will you regret it when the time of testing comes, you will not be prepared to be an encouragement for the Lord to others. God's training ground is behind the front lines – take advantage of it.

When I was on a school board, a very controversial meeting was on the agenda. We were going to write a policy for librarians regarding the selection of quality books to ensure that obscene materials would not be purchased.

I had been in prayer and fasting all week and had asked several churches to pray. The Lord had guided me in the writing of the policy and showed me that by using the word "obscene" instead of "pornographic," and defining it, very few people would insist that a policy was a problem. Up until this point in history (mid 1980's) there was a huge debate, even in the Supreme Court, with regard to the definition of pornography.

Earlier in the day, I needed to be at a meeting with the district office, but they were running late. I told them I would wait in the boardroom. While I was sitting there in the peace and quiet, the Lord spoke to my heart and said, "Don't just sit there. Get up and pray throughout this room."

I proceeded to walk up and down every row of chairs, touching each one, and praying for God's angels to be in that meeting that night. Usually the press, along with the opposition, sat in the first two rows, making it very difficult to focus.

I remember boldly proclaiming that only supporters would sit in those rows and that the opposition would sit to the back. To my amazement, that evening the opposition was in the far back corner, the press was to the side, and only Christians were in the two front rows.

The policy passed smoothly with very limited opposition. The week of prayer and fasting by me and others and the prayer in the board room that day allowed God to have the victory.

Whine or Wine?

For the time being no discipline brings joy, but seems grievous and painful; but afterwards it yields a peaceable fruit of righteousness to those who have been trained by it (a harvest of fruit which consists in righteousness—to God's will in purpose, thought, and action, resulting in right living and right standing with God).

Hebrews 12:11

Since the late 1990's, the Lord has been speaking to my heart, "It's the Season of the Grapes," and I've also heard in my spirit, "It's Time." I have been so consumed with the vision of grapes, that I have paintings and images of them throughout my home.

When I researched grapes in the Bible, all I could find was the "crushing of the grapes" and a "winepress." It seemed like such a harsh visual.

I thought to myself, "certainly the grapes must be a symbol for the time of the harvest - the end times - not a time of crushing." Perhaps there will be a "crushing" on the world and many will turn to God.

But before that happens, God has to prepare His saints to bring in the great harvest and His bride, the church, must be ready for His return. He does that through pressure, and this pressure creates the wine in our lives. Hebrews 12:6 says, "Whom the Lord loves He chastens . . ." (NKJV).

When the unbelievers in the world see Christians, they need to see the peace and the joy of God. If we are whining and complaining under pressure, then we are no different than the world.

When you feel the pressure of God's hand upon you, learn from it, and let God have His perfect work. Remember, that when you feel weak, "the joy of the Lord is your strength" (Nehemiah 8:10, NASB).

The yoke of God is "light" and not heavy because it is for our good and not for our crushing. It produces the FRUITS of the Spirit.

It is TIME for you to allow God to develop the fruits of the Spirit in you - "love, joy, peace, patience, kindness, goodness, faithfulness, gentleness, and self-control" (Galatians 5:22, NASB). Let God turn the grapes in your life into wine that can be poured out to others.

The Victory Is Already Ours

Jesus came with them to a place called Gethsemane, and He said to His disciples..."Remain here and keep watch with Me."

Matthew 26:36, 38 NASB

Often when I think of the victory we have in life because of Jesus, I think about how he defeated Satan in the wilderness, cast out demons, rebuked the storm, and of course, rose from the dead. I often forget the time He spent in Gethsemane. Jesus, the Son of God, was confident He would not be touched by Satan, but Jesus, the Son of Man, had to resist the enemy in the garden not for His sake, but for the sake of all humankind, or it would have never been possible for us to become sons of God.

When the world becomes more than you can endure, think about what Jesus bore in Gethsemane and know that "He has overcome the world" for our sake.

I have a pastor/friend who reminds me to not rejoice that we have authority over the devil, but to remind the devil that Jesus has authority over him. My friend has taught me to quote in prayer Jude 9: "But when (even) the archangel Michael, contending with the devil...he dared not (presume to) bring an abusive condemnation against him, but (simply) said, 'The Lord rebuke you!'"

After the rebuke, begin to praise and thank Jesus for what He did for you in the wilderness, in Gethsemane, and on the cross. Thank Him for His precious blood that was shed for you, and the enemy will flee.

Are you focused on an unanswered prayer and feeling discouraged? Focus on the promise of eternal life and rejoice over those answered prayers of Jesus when He prayed in the garden for victory and triumph on your behalf.

The School of Adversity

Be strong in the Lord (be empowered through your union with Him); draw
your strength from Him (that strength which His boundless might provides).
Ephesians 6:10

We must come to a point in our faith when we are not just interested in His blessings, but of knowing God Himself. One of the toughest things for a new believer to learn is that we will go through some tough times in order to fully understand the power and love of God.

Some Christians get angry with God, not understanding that "His ways are not our ways" (Isaiah 55: 8). God's plan is not yet clear.

I recently re-read a letter I received from a pastor in 1991. He wrote:

"We, like you, have also been taught in the wilderness. As you know, my family has been through some violent storms. My wife's first husband died in the pulpit; our first-born died at birth; and our Benjamin was born dead, but God raised him up during ten days of intensive care. Through it all we saw that God brings the beauty of nature after the storms of life.

The irregular beauty of the mountain is begotten in the storm, and the heroes of life are born in the sweeping storms of battle. God has a purpose in the storm and the battle. The Lord clears the way for us through the giant waves, the deep dark clouds, and the tumultuous storms. The sorrow, grief and pain have brought us to new heights of peace. 'In quietness and confidence shall be your strength.' 'Weeping may endure for the night, but joy comes in the morning.'

We have indeed been left broken, weary, and beaten down in the valley, but God has brought a richer, deeper, and a more abiding manhood and womanhood. The Lord invariably gets His greatest victories out of the most apparent defeats. It takes great sorrow, defeat and despair to widen the soul. The Lord never really uses anyone to any great degree until after He has broken him or her in the school of adversity. Tribulation is the real path to victory and triumph."

How do we endure such tribulation? Paul wrote when he was in prison, "I have learned in any and all circumstances the secret of facing every situation, whether well fed or going hungry, having a sufficiency and enough to spare, or going without and being in want. I have strength for all things in Christ Who empowers me (I am ready for anything and equal to anything through him Who infuses inner strength into me; I am self-sufficient in Christ's sufficiency)" (Philippians 4:13-14). We lean on Jesus.

You Are Not Alone

Cast your burden on the Lord (releasing the weight of it) and He will sustain you; He will never allow the (consistently) righteous to be moved (made to slip, fall, or fail).

Psalm 55: 22

I asked for guidance from the Holy Spirit as to what I should tell the people through this devotion. He said to tell them, "You are not alone." He said, "Tell them to come to Me when they are overwhelmed."

If you have given your life to the Lord completely, then you know, as I know, that He gives each person a portion of responsibility according to what He believes we can handle.

I have many pages in my journal writings where I give back to Him the burdens of life that He seems to require of me. On one page I wrote, "The details and tasks in my life are sometimes overwhelming. Lately, a few things have dropped through the cracks and I need your support and help."

I then listed six things that were overwhelming me. Later I went back and discovered that every single one of them had been taken care of.

On another journal page I wrote, "I need help with the small things - the 100 details of my life. I think I would have done better as a pioneer woman chopping wood and facing the challenges of the Wild West, than handling the stress of a woman in leadership in the 21st century. I need you Lord and can't do this without you."

When I look back at the change and transition I was going through in those stressful times, there were not any major miracles that took place, except the miracle of me making it through to the other side with His peace and presence. Without depending on Christ as our burden-bearer, we will be lonely, weary, discouraged, burned-out, or exhausted.

You are not really letting go of your burden when you cast it upon the Lord. You are putting the responsibility of the burden and YOURSELF in His hands, and it suddenly becomes lighter.

"Those who hope in the Lord will renew their strength. They will soar on wings like eagles; they will run and not grow weary, they will walk and not be faint" (Isaiah 40:31, NIV).

The Lord impressed on my heart "To tell all my people that have been called by Him that He will give them the wisdom and strength they need to complete the assignments God has given them." He put on my heart that there is going to be a great outpouring of wisdom and strength on His leadership called by Him in these last days and not to fear the responsibility.

"For I know the thoughts and plans I have for you, says the Lord, thoughts and plans for welfare and peace and not for evil, to give you hope in your final outcome" (Jeremiah 29:11). Come to Him with your burdens and be in His peace and presence today.

Not One Day Late

Though it tarry, wait (earnestly) for it, because it will surely come; it will not be behindhand on its appointed day.

Habakkuk 2: 3

Habakkuk had come to the Lord in frustration and fear and asked God, "Why are you silent when the wicked one destroys him who is more righteous than the oppressor is? Why do you make men defenseless against their foes? Will our enemies slay nations forever?"

Habakkuk was the "burden-bearer" – the praying prophet during times of challenge on God's people. He witnessed the decline and fall of the Assyrian empire and the rise of the Babylonian kingdom. Habakkuk had observed the leaders in Judah oppressing the poor, and so he asks God how long He will allow these wicked leaders to prosper.

God reminds Habakkuk that the just shall live by faith in God and to have confidence that God is doing what is right. He then assures Habakkuk that ultimately righteousness and justice will come in due time and will prevail for the people of God.

Habakkuk then breaks forth into a song of praise to calm his own personal fears and problems. At one point in this dialogue, Habakkuk apologizes to God for complaining against Him.

God responds, "Write the vision and engrave it so plainly upon tablets that everyone who passes may (be able to) read (it easily and quickly) as he hastens by. For the vision is yet for an appointed time and it hastens to the end (fulfillment); it will not deceive or disappoint" (Habakkuk 2:2-3).

Does any of this sound familiar in our marketplace lives? Controlling or incapable managers, delayed promotions, evil people prospering, and nations or companies ruled by the ungodly? Do our own personal visions seem delayed?

How can we use Habakkuk as an example in our own waiting and stretching times? First, it is okay to talk to God about your fears, frustrations, and disappointments (Habakkuk did for two full chapters!) as long as you get to the next phase.

Second, build your faith by recalling all the great things God has done for you in the past, and thank Him for those victories. Habakkuk went all the way back to God parting the Red Sea and the deliverance of His people from the horses and the chariots.

Third, Habakkuk renewed the promise and the vision God had given Him and spoke God's promises before they came to past, trusting God's Word more than the circumstances before him.

Fourth, Habakkuk understood the principle of "nevertheless." Habakkuk proclaims, "Though the fig tree does not blossom and there is no fruit on the vines, (though) the product of the olive fails and the fields yield no food, though the flock is cut off from the fold and there are no cattle in the stalls, yet, I will rejoice in the Lord; I will exult in the (victorious) God of my salvation!" (Habakkuk 3:17-18).

Finally, Habakkuk rose above the circumstances, operating in the fullness of God's peace and joy. "The Lord God is my Strength, my personal bravery, and my invincible army; He makes my feet like hinds' feet and will make me to walk (not to stand still in terror, but to walk) and make (spiritual) progress upon my high places (of trouble, suffering, or responsibility)!" (Habakkuk 3:19).

Renewed Vitality

Salt is good (an excellent thing), but if salt has lost its strength and has become saltless (insipid, flat), how shall its saltiness be restored?
Luke 14: 34

Workplace organizations often talk about team vitality and synergy (group energy). When teams first start on projects they have vision and excitement, but as challenges arise and personalities clash, they suffer burnout and eventually just go through the motions without the passion.

This can also happen in our relationship with God. We get in a rut of going through spiritual routines or being satisfied with our spiritual growth.

I remember as a young Christian, thinking I had finally mastered the fruit of the Spirit "patience" (big mistake). Then my children turned into teenagers, and I discovered my sin nature all over again!

If we stop at a certain stage of growth and make major assumptions that "we have arrived," we are in danger of developing a spiritual pride and becoming a target for the enemy's attacks. Even specific times of the day to read the Bible and pray, can lack vitality. God may interrupt your schedule just to show you that you are worshipping the habit instead of Him. Has it become your time alone with God or your time alone with your habit?

When I get to a dry place and realize I am in a routine instead of a relationship, I stop and press in to find out what is wrong. I go through a process of self-examination and discover what new dimension or qualities God wants to add to my life before I move forward.

When teams lose vitality in organizations, it is necessary to go back to the drawing board to work out any personal issues or frustrations; renew the vision so they have purpose and direction again; and examine if they are headed in the right direction or if any improvements or changes need to take place.

Are you stuck in your prayer and Bible study time? Are your spiritual habits losing life and vitality?

Stop immediately! And talk to God to see if there is a new direction He wants to give you, or perhaps He wants you to immerse your habit in His love and presence and bring in His vitality.

I have a friend that I used to pray with every Wednesday morning at 6:30 a.m. There have been times that these prayers were powerful, anointed, and quickly answered. Just when we thought we had this prayer time "down pat," something happened to my schedule. However, God, in His wisdom, wants to confound the devil, and He would have us spontaneously pray at other times – the night before, the next afternoon, in the car running an errand, or by e-mail communication.

We continued to do our best to keep a spiritual habit, but God worked to keep His vitality, His timing, His spontaneity, and His presence in our prayer times. In fact, He has expanded our prayer times out to other people.

Do you need your salt restored? Come to Him, and let Him refresh and renew it.

Jesus, Our Floodgate

Who shall separate us from the love of Christ?

Romans 8:35 NIV

Apostle Paul continued that neither "trouble, hardship, persecution, famine, nakedness, danger, sword" can separate us from the love of Christ (Romans 8: 35).

Isaiah told the people of God, "When you pass through the waters, I will be with you; and through the rivers, they will not overflow you. When you walk through the fire, you will not be scorched, nor will the flame burn upon you" (Isaiah 43: 2, NASB).

In the *Parable of the Seed,* Jesus warned to never allow the tribulations of the world to keep you from remembering that God loves you. Jesus never promised to stop the floods from coming; He only promised He would be our floodgate that keeps the flood from overwhelming us. His love is with us, and He will not forsake us.

When my workload and responsibilities seem overwhelming to me, God likes to remind me how blessed we are in America to have our jobs and our homes. In 2005, I had a short conversation with a Christian international student from Ivory Coast, Africa.

Even through he seemed positive and happy, in my spirit I could tell that something was troubling him. When I pressed in to see how he really was, I discovered that he had a close friend in Africa who was being forced out of his home along with his wife and child, because he lost his job and could not pay the $50.00 rent.

My friend told me that it was very bad in his country and that people struggle to provide food and housing for their families. My African friend has very little income from a part-time job at the college campus, yet he had been sending almost all his money to family members and his friend to help them survive.

On the day I was talking to him, he was carrying a heavy burden for his Christian brother-in-the-Lord and trying to figure out how he could get the rent money to him. I tell you this next part for inspiration, not for any personal recognition, because my faith is small compared to my

African brothers and sisters. I drove my friend to Western Union immediately and wired $150 to Africa for two-months rent and food for this family.

I drove my friend to Western Union requires that you pose a question and an answer for the recipient of the money (a password). When my friend was asked, "What question do you want us to ask?" He replied, "What is Jesus to you?" When Western Union asked, what should the recipient answer, he replied, "He is the Savior of my Soul." These two young men, living on pocket change, trusting God from week to week for His provision, could not be separated from the love of Christ.

Later, a woman read this devotion. She was so grateful for her new home, she asked God how she could bless someone else. The Lord put on her heart to send this man in Africa $50 every month for his rent, and she was faithful to support this family every month for a year.

The following year, a few Christians sent this young man enough money to start his own business (a coffee shop) so that he can become independent. I marvel at how much God loves this young man in Africa and meets all his needs. Surely, we can believe that God will meet all our needs, too.

Going On With Jesus

You are those who have remained (throughout) and persevered with me in my trials.

Luke 22:28

Multiple times I have said to Jesus, "There is no way you could understand this trial or temptation. When did you have to manage difficult projects? When did you have to multi-task or deal with new technologies? When did you fight bumper to bumper traffic?"

I may sound disrespectful and full of self-pity, but I was reaching out to Jesus in times of defeat and weariness, trying to believe He truly understood what I was going through in 21st century management. Of course, as I study the Scripture, I see that Jesus had long sleepless nights, disciples who challenged Him, people who hated Him, throngs of people pressing in on Him from every side, very few quiet times, and limited finances!

There is no trial or temptation to us that Jesus does not know and understand. The question is are we trying to shield ourselves from these challenges, avoid them, or run away from them? Are we changing jobs, because it is God's will, or because we do not like the circumstances?

It is God who may be allowing or engineering the circumstances to build strength and character in us. He has walked this path, faced these temptations, and now we are walking this path with Him. The challenges we face are challenges to the life of Christ in us.

There have been many times over the years that it seemed I lost God's favor in the workplace. "Needles in the nest" have often been an indication to me that it is time to move on and "take flight."

Now I can see that the trials were of Him, because I had some weak areas of not trusting Him that He needed to strengthen. The circumstances were to prepare me for His calling on my life, and I could have missed a great learning opportunity.

When God intends for me "to go through" and not "go around," I press into His presence for wisdom, skill, and strength. In those moments, I feel centered and sense God's control of my life. As for the skill it takes to manage the challenging circumstances, "I can do all things through Christ who strengthens me" (Philippians 4:13, NKJV).

The next time you face a challenge, do not take flight or go around. Try going on with Jesus.

The Valley of Humiliation

*My grace (My favor and loving-kindness and mercy) is enough for you
(sufficient against any danger and enables you to bear the trouble manfully);
for My strength and power are made perfect (fulfilled and completed) and
show themselves most effective in (your) weakness.*

2 Corinthians 12:9

Living in the valley of humiliation is living in the drab every day life,
barely recalling the last exhilarating experience you had with God. Even
deeper in the valley of humiliation are those times that you failed in your
finances, lost a job, lost your temper, or lost a ministry. The humiliation
makes us feel unworthy and weak.

In those times we tend to become depressed and turn away from God
in shame. We forget that He brought us to that place so that we can
depend on Him.

Apostle Paul had a humiliation – a thorn in the flesh. Most scholars
believe that the "thorn" was his poor eyesight – something very
humiliating for a writer and for a man that believed in healing. I
personally believe that Scripture indicates it was the constant persecution,
beatings, and arrests he went through that became his thorn in the side.

Paul called the thorn, "a messenger of Satan to torment me" (2
Corinthians 12:7, NASB). In the same letter to the Corinthians, he
wrote, "I have…been in prison more frequently, been flogged more
severely, and been exposed to death again and again. Five times I received
from the Jews the forty lashes minus one. Three times I was beaten with
rods, once I was stoned, three times I was shipwrecked, I spent a night
and a day in the open sea, I have been constantly on the move. I have
been in danger from rivers, in danger from bandits, in danger from my
own countrymen, in danger from Gentiles; in danger in the city, in
danger in the country, in danger at sea; and in danger from false brothers.
I have labored and toiled and have often gone without sleep; I have
known hunger and thirst and have often gone without food; I have been
cold and naked" (NIV).

Paul's physical wounds from the beatings and having to complete his
prison terms must have slowed down his ministry to a great extent. I do

not think he cried out to God, "Could you please heal my eyes, this is so humiliating!" I think he called upon God three times to "get Satan off his back!"

Imagine the humiliation of this person who proclaimed God's goodness and then appeared to lack God's favor. Paul explains to his followers, that God allowed it "to keep me from becoming conceited" (2 Corinthians 12:7, NIV).

Paul tells his followers, "I will all the more gladly glory in my weaknesses and infirmities, that the strength and power of Christ (the Messiah) may rest (yes, may pitch a tent over and dwell) upon me!" (2 Corinthians 12:9). Paul then confirms that it was the hardships and persecutions that he wanted to stop when he wrote, "So for the sake of Christ, I am well pleased and take pleasure in infirmities, insults, hardships, persecutions, perplexities and distresses; for when I am weak (in human strength), then am I (truly) strong (able, powerful in divine strength)." (v. 10).

People may want to know about our God who gives us mountaintop experiences, favor and blessing, but they will also want to know our God, because they see we are overcomers – full of peace, joy, and God's grace – in times of difficulty and humiliating circumstances. They want to know how we deal with our greatest fears.

A Broken Heart

Do you not know that your body is a temple of the Holy Spirit...? You are not your own...

1 Corinthians 6:19 NASB

When I ran for school board in 1985, in obedience to the Lord's call, I suffered great persecution and the pain of rejection. Pastors did not agree with me; Christians called to criticize me. Teachers humiliated my children in three different schools, and the news media harassed me on a daily basis.

I was a young mother, scared, but not defeated, because God was very near to me and clear in His direction. After winning the election, the persecution and pressure continued.

I could not walk into a grocery store without someone voicing if they were for me or against me. There were people in opposition who said for years, "I hate Wendy Flint," and one father forbade his daughter to date my son.

The greatest pain of all came the fourth year of my school board service when it became clear that other members on the board did not want me to run again. Being rejected by those who you thought were your comrades is the greatest rejection of all.

For many months the pain of my broken heart of not running for office again, combined with all the persecution, grew with intensity. Even in the pain, I continued to go out and teach other parents how to win school board elections, stand for what was right for children, and pray for their public schools.

One day, the pain in my heart was so great; I cried out to the Lord, "Please take this pain away!"

He replied, "I can't."

I said, "You mean, you won't?"

He said, "I can't, because through the pain, there is a great anointing that pours forth to others and gives them the boldness and courage to take a stand for what is right and pure. It is the anointing of your pain that is breaking the yoke of fear and setting people free."

At that moment, I no longer belonged to myself and I accepted all that God had in His will for me to accomplish. It is a very deep mystery to understand that God can accomplish His purpose in this world through a broken heart. The pain of what you are going through now may not make sense, but if our pain sets others free someday, then we have been used mightily by God, and we are victorious over the enemy.

The Long Road Home

Whatever may be your task, work at it heartily, as (something done) for the Lord and not for men, knowing (with all certainty) that it is from the Lord (and not from men) that you will receive the inheritance which is your (real) reward. (The one Whom) you are actually serving (is) the Lord Christ (the Messiah).

Colossians 3:23-24

Suffering is not a pleasant topic. In fact, in the religion I was raised in, you were not allowed to confess any suffering and only "think positive thoughts." Having a positive attitude is powerful, but denial of circumstances can create stress and illness.

During the "faith movement" of the 1970's, if you were suffering, Christians would judge you for not having enough faith or not having God's favor. The alarms went off for me immediately on that doctrinal belief, because it had the same "ring" as the guilt-driven rules of the false religion I was taught as a child.

Jesus said that there would be suffering in the world, but that He overcame the world. He promised to be with us and not forsake us. He promised to send the Comforter and to answer our prayers, but He never promised that there would be no testing or trials.

So why is there suffering? It enables us to understand what takes place in the lives of others and makes us better ministers of the Gospel. Whether we overcome a trial or succeed in having peace in the midst of trying circumstances, it is the "how" we overcame that we share with others.

We are often tempted to believe that if circumstances do not result in benefiting us, that we have somehow lost the blessing of God or that we are being punished. In many situations, Christians develop an anger or resentment toward God because of the loss of a job, a divorce, rejection, or loss of a loved one.

Most suffering is a part of our every day life, and it is our faith and trust in God that gets us through. There is some suffering allowed by God that is part of His plan for our life. He gives us training lessons to equip us for His purpose.

If you read my journal, you will see where I often cried out to God to remove me from a job because of challenges. It never happened until I accepted with joy His purpose for my life.

Instead of letting me escape the pressure, He strengthened my spiritual muscles. Now when I am in the midst of challenging situations, I am not moved, I stay calm, I hold my ground, I wait upon the Lord, I confront the issue when required, and I go forward in a God-designed courageous way with truth and assurance.

We have heard it before – suffering builds character. In the workplace – it builds leadership qualities. Instead of shortcuts, God's intention is for us to take the long road back home to Him.

His Highest Goals

He said, "Take now your son…"

Genesis 22:2

If you have children, you know that the ultimate sacrifice is to trust God with your children and literally give them to Him for His will, not ours.

I recently met a woman who lost her seven year-old to pneumonia two years ago. After all the medical research in this world, you would think we could stop a child from dying of pneumonia. Her best friend had previously lost a child, and this woman's constant prayer was, "Please God, don't ever make me go through that."

The Scripture, "Take now your son," in Genesis, refers to Abraham being asked to put his son on the altar. Abraham did not have a choice in the sacrifice that would prove his obedience to the Lord. Abraham neither argued nor conferred with God, but simply obeyed.

The trial this woman went through was horrific, but she had a peace and said, "My husband now serves the Lord, and my two oldest sons are both in the ministry. They all admit that his death changed their lives forever."

It is not my intent to debate the theory of pre-destination or if God allowed this woman's son to die. I do know from the Scripture that suffering is still in the world, and that God gives us victory in our suffering and works things out for good for those who love the Lord. Bad things happen to good people, and Satan still roams the earth seeking whom he can devour.

Ultimately, God uses all of our trials to bring us closer to Him and to transform us into His image. His ways are not our ways – but His highest goals need to become our goals.

When you go through challenges, you will have to decide: 1) Do I defend myself? 2) Do I leave the situation or job? 3) Do I deal with it as in prayer? 4) Do I accept it as a trial and allow God's purpose and growth in me to become complete? 5) Do I do more than one of the above choices, or perhaps all of them?

Each individual will only know through prayer and communion with God. One thing I am sure of – nothing can separate us from the love of God.

A Surpassing Peace

Peace I leave with you; My peace give unto you...do not let your heart be troubled.

John 14:27

Knowing God is knowing that He honors His Word. It is impossible for God to lie. When we move from believing into "knowing," we move into the peace of God.

If Jesus said He will not forsake us, then when we face hostile or overwhelming circumstances, we can be confident that He will be in our midst offering us peace. Our responsibility is to refuse to be troubled (resist the enemy of doubt) and receive God's gift of Peace.

In the 1970's, when my husband Terry and I had three small children, we needed to purchase a larger home. We were living in a 900 square foot house in Washington State. A Christian couple owned the home we wanted to purchase, and they said that God instructed them to sell it to us, even though our offer was not the best one.

Our real estate agent took us to meet some underwriters at a bank to see if we could persuade them to give us a loan. I was not employed and Terry had only been on his job for three months. When we left the meeting, the agent told us that he had never seen anything more impossible for getting a home loan than our situation and that it was not hopeful.

Standing on the sidewalk, in front of the bank, I responded, "That's wonderful!" He gave me a very puzzled look. I continued, "My Lord has told the people who own this home, and He has told us that this home is ours. If it is impossible, then all of us, including you, are going to see God work a miracle in this situation, and He will receive all the glory. I can't wait to see what God is going to do!"

One of the things the bank told us was that Terry had to make more money. I had just read a Scripture that week that said, "Promotions come from the Lord." I encouraged Terry to go talk to his boss. He did, and the boss gave him exactly what we needed.

The agent said, "That's only one of many things that you will have to overcome." Five days later, the board of the bank met and approved our loan. The agent said that he had never witnessed anything like it, and he recognized that it had to be faith.

Romans 4:21 says, "Being fully persuaded that God had power to do what He had promised" (NIV). Are you fully persuaded? Are you at complete peace in your situation?

If not, then find Scriptures in God's Word that assure you of things that are true, but not yet seen. Keep reading them until you grab hold of that peace. Get God's promises into your spirit until your "knower" knows that God is a good God, and He is working on your behalf.

That kind of peace, my friend, is the peace that the Scripture promises, "transcends all understanding shall garrison and mount guard over your hearts and minds in Christ Jesus" (Philippians 4:7).

Look to God

Look to Me, and be saved...

Isaiah 45: 22 NKJV

I read a story about a man who was trapped in an airplane that was on fire. Everyone around him was cursing God, but he decided to praise him loudly above the cries. There was an opening in the plane that he was suddenly supernaturally pulled through, and he found himself safe on the ground.

I thought to myself, what would I do in a crisis situation like that, cry and curse, or praise God? I had an opportunity to find out.

One August day, I stepped incorrectly on the corner of our swimming pool, twisted my leg, severely bent my foot, and fell backwards into the water. I had a big terrycloth robe on and the weight of it filled with water took me immediately to the bottom of the pool. I had to come out of the robe to get to the top of the water, and as I pushed to the top there was an excruciating pain in my right knee, lower leg and foot.

I hit the surface screaming in pain. Fear wanted to grip me immediately, because I knew there was something severely wrong with my leg, but I also instinctively knew I needed to praise God immediately. As I dog-paddled across the water, crawled out of the pool and across the patio inches at a time, I exclaimed, "Thank you, God, for healing my leg! Thank you, God, for healing my leg! In Jesus' name, help me!"

I managed to get in the house, wrap a blanket around me, and pull myself up into a recliner chair. I called my daughter who lived five houses away and asked her to call an ambulance.

Over and over, I kept saying, "Thank you, God, for healing my leg! I praise Your mighty name! You are Lord of my life and this situation."

Paramedics thought my leg was broken and braced it for the ambulance ride to the hospital. When the emergency room doctor moved my foot, I cried in anguish. The doctor said, "I'm pretty sure you have a broken foot and a torn ligament in your knee," and he sent me off to x-ray.

While waiting in the hallway for x-ray, I had one last conversation with God. I asked Him if He would spare me from having a cast on my leg and allow me to go back to work. Then I continued to praise Him. I felt His peace. When the doctor looked at the x-ray, he was surprised, shook his head, and said, "I could have sworn that foot was broken, but I don't see any damage at all."

When he moved my foot again, there was no pain. It took ten days for my knee to heal enough to go back to work (a pretty speedy recovery considering), and when I left the hospital there was no more pain in my foot.

Some may ask, "Why didn't God heal your knee?" My reply is, "He did!" He healed my foot instantly, and my knee in ten days.

What comes out of your mouth when you face a trial? Are you proclaiming fear or faith? I believe I reacted the way I did because I had spent so much time in His Word, and His promises were deep inside of me like a living well that I could draw from.

Part 4

Hearing from God

The Friendship of God

*The Lord would speak to Moses face to face, as a man speaks with his
friend...*

Exodus 33:11 NIV

My 30-year old daughter tells others, "My mother is my best friend."
That was not always the case. There were years of pouring out instruction
and discipline to "train her in the way (she) should go" (Proverbs 22:6,
NIV).

Even though we now share a close friendship, there are times she still
needs her "mother" as she learns to raise her own children. Just as our
human relationships change over time, our relationship with the Lord
should be growing so that God becomes both our father and friend.

Bruce Wilkinson in *Secrets of the Vine* writes about the importance of
an abiding friendship with the Lord, "Unless your friendship with God
becomes your first priority, you will never fulfill your true destiny as a
Christian or a leader."

Many believers ask me, "How do you get direction from the Lord?"
Most of my decisions are made because of the peace-filled daily walk I
strive to have with Him.

If I am reading His Word and walking in conversation and prayer
with my Lord, I can trust that commonsense thoughts, direction, and
creative inspirations are from Him.

God communicates from His Spirit to our spirit. Jesus said we need
spiritual ears and eyes to perceive the will of the Lord. The Bible says that
we, as Christians, have been given the "mind of Christ" (1 Corinthians
2:16), and God gave us a spirit "of power and of love and of calm and
well-balanced mind..." (II Timothy 1: 7).

God's messages transfer from our spirits to our minds, where we
translate them into our language. His messages then become thoughts in
our heads along with feelings of confirmation in our spirits.

"Delight yourself also in the Lord, and He will give you the desires
and secret petitions of your heart. Commit your way to the Lord; (roll

and repose each care of your load on Him); trust (lean on, rely on, and be confident) also in Him and He will bring it to pass" (Psalm 37: 4-5).

I believe that God placed the secret desires of our heart within us. This is why we get that sense that what we are doing is God's will for us.

If you find yourself lacking the confidence to go forward with your plans, know this: in your friendship with God, if your decisions are wrong, He will lovingly produce a sense of restraint and warning. Once He does, you must stop immediately.

What is the worse case scenario? You step out in a direction you believe to be correct for your life, and you get a warning signal in your spirit – a loss of peace in your soul. You step back and wait.

Nothing is gained, but nothing is lost. God does not expect us to learn this without testing and trying!

I counsel people, "If you are right with God, if you have been in prayer, if you are not hearing or feeling a 'no' in your spirit, then go with what is in your heart, and trust that the Lord (who is in your heart) put it there. Until you test the waters, you will never know."

On the other hand, if you DID receive a clear direction from God, and forces of resistance come at you as soon as you step out, that is also a good sign that you are in His will, and you need to keep pushing through to what He called you to do.

Unanswered Prayer

What man is there among you who, when his son asks for a loaf (of bread), will give him a stone?

Matthew 7:9 NASB

The day I wrote this devotion, I awoke at 4:30 a.m., and the Lord spoke to my heart and said, "I want to talk about unanswered prayer. Tell my children to not give up."

Unanswered prayer is not about God – it is usually about us. We are quick to believe that if we do not get what we ask for, then it must not be God's will.

What we need to do first is check out our relationship with Him. In Ephesians 4:26-27, the Apostle Paul admonishes us, "In your anger do not sin: do not let the sun go down while you are still angry, and do not give the devil a foothold" (NIV).

Anger with friends, family, or co-workers could be blocking the flow of God's blessing in our lives. Another prayer block can be any unwillingness to forgive someone. Christ strongly emphasizes in Matthew 6: 14-15 that God will not allow us to have good fellowship with Him until we have forgiven others.

Does our attitude say to God, "I know I have been irritable; I know I am angry at my spouse; I know I need to forgive that person, but I still need you to bless me!" Rather than being defiant with our Father God, we need to surrender, admit where we are wrong, and ask for forgiveness.

We need to turn the flashlight on our hearts to make sure there is nothing blocking the reception of God's love, because Jesus says, regarding His followers, "Everyone who asks receives . . ." (Matthew 7: 8, NASB).

If the heart is clear, the next thing to do when waiting for answered prayer is to press in and pray for grace to continue to trust Him in the midst of your circumstances. There is sometimes a purpose for our struggles and problems, and God wants to use them to build endurance in our lives.

Even when the Apostle Paul struggled with his "thorn in the flesh,"

God said, "My grace is sufficient for you, for my power is made perfect in weakness" (2 Corinthians 12:9, NIV). God was saying to hang in there – I will give you the strength to endure, and I will be there at the end of this trial to meet all your needs.

Waiting for answered prayer builds character and faith. Having all your prayers instantly answered will not grow you in your faith.

Also know, He does not want you to stop asking and seeking just because the answer is slow in coming. "Keep on asking and it will be given you; keep on seeking and you will find; keep on knocking (reverently) and (the door) will be opened to you. For everyone who keeps on asking receives; and he who keeps on seeking finds; and to him who keeps on knocking, (the door) will be opened" (Matthew 7:7-8).

Finally, God encouraged me with the message, "You will not possess what you do not pursue." God does expect us to take action.

When we are praying for something that we believe God directed us toward, then we need to step out in faith and try different doors until the right one opens. A closed door does not mean "no" – it means "not now" or perhaps "try a different path."

Psalm 84:11 says, "No good thing does HE withhold from those walk uprightly" (NASB). God wants you to not give up. Breakthrough is on the way.

He Talks

He calls his own... by name...

John 10:3

I did not know about having a conversation with the Lord when I was a child raised in Christian Science. I was told that I could not talk to God, and He could not talk to me.

I longed for God to know me and always felt sad inside that we could not communicate. I used to look up into heaven with tears in my eyes and say nothing, because I knew He could not hear.

There was such a struggle between the truth I sensed in my heart and the facts that I was being told. When I did go to the altar of a Methodist church to find out who this Jesus was and to receive forgiveness, I heard the Lord so loud in my spirit, I thought the pastor had said something to me.

When I opened my eyes, I saw that the pastor was not in front of me. I heard the Lord say, "Wendy, I love you, I forgive you, and I am so glad you have come unto me."

The startling realization that God could talk and that He called me by my name caused me to run out of the church overwhelmed with emotion. It was my first visit to this small country church, and I am sure they were wondering, "Who was that?"

There wasn't even an altar call that day – there was simply a communion service, and the pastor was reading about the Blood of the Lamb and how Christ died for our sins. The mention of the name of Jesus and His forgiveness brought me to my knees that Sunday morning, and the scales fell off my eyes.

All I could say over and over again when I left the church, "He talks. He talks. And He talked to me!"

I am aware that not many Christians have had such a dramatic experience, and I struggle with telling the story. In my case, I am not so sure I could have seen the light in my darkness without the experience.

I would say to others who were raised Christian or have always known Christ, "You are so blessed to have known Him your whole life." The disciples of Jesus said, "We have seen the Lord," but Thomas said, "Unless I see...I will not believe" (John 20:25, NASB). Thomas needed the personal touch of Jesus.

When Thomas did see the Lord and touch Him, he said to Him, "My Lord and my God!" (John 20:28), and I am sure he never doubted again.

As a result of a personal touch from God, I was delivered from a great darkness, and my husband and I were both saved from a long lineage of unbelievers. We became first generation Christians, raising our children in the faith.

Religious doctrine will fail you but a personal relationship with Jesus will endure. Whatever your salvation experience, whether by simple trust and faith in His word or through a dramatic revelation, I encourage you to develop a personal relationship with Jesus Christ.

Become intimate with Him in prayer and conversation so that nothing can ever shake your faith in the future. Do not take communication with God for granted.

Learn from this "child" who lived in silence for over 20 years, and then learned the awesome realization that God hears our prayers and talks to our hearts. I am still in awe that this God of the universe calls us by name.

In your workplace situations today, lean on this awesome God.

My Sheep Hear My Voice

Elijah went up by a whirlwind into heaven. And Elisha...saw him no more.
2 Kings 2: 11-12

Elijah, a powerful prophet, was Elisha's mentor and father figure, and his sudden departure into heaven must have created a great sense of vulnerability and loneliness. All of us have had Elijah's in our lives that were there for every bend and turn in the road to guide and council us.

When that person departed for whatever reason, we thought we could not go on, but we did. Others have had Elijah experiences directly from God, but they do not last forever, because God intends for us to walk by faith.

Being alone without your Elijah means wishing that someone else would take the initiative and responsibility, but in the end you know you must step out and do it yourself.

It may even mean separation of fellowship with others for a season, because others would only distract you from your mission. Being alone without your Elijah means walking through the refining fire, not knowing the final outcome and resisting taking flight in another direction.

I think my entire walk with God has been an effort on His part to make me recognize He is always there, even when I am not experiencing Him. I was raised by parents in a false religion and was told, "You cannot talk to God, and He cannot talk to you."

They gave me an image of a 'spiritual blanket' that covered the earth – sort of an energy shield or force – rather than an image of a Father that loved me. Due to this huge void in my life, God made Himself very real to me, and I wanted to experience Jesus forever.

He, on the other hand, wanted me to develop a relationship with Him where I knew through His Word and His faithfulness that He was always present. This was the relationship Jesus had with God on earth.

Laurie Beth Jones writes in *Jesus CEO,* "Jesus had a sense of companionship with the divine source of his being, a source that not only knew him intimately but cared for him as well." Jones believes that this sense of God's love drove Jesus, especially on his darker days. His desire to please His Father and to return to His personal embrace again drove Him to do God's will.

In the book, *Hinds' Feet on High Places* by Hannah Hurnard, there is a portion of the journey for Much Afraid that is called the *Shores of Loneliness*. The Good Shepherd tells her at the shore of a great sea,

> *"It is now time for Me to leave you, Much Afraid, and to return to the mountains. Remember, even though you seem to be farther away than ever from the High Places (the Elijah experiences) and from Me, there is really no distance at all separating us. I can cross the desert sands as swiftly as I can leap from the High Places to the valleys, and whenever you call for Me, I shall come. This is the word I now leave with you. Believe it and practice it with joy. My sheep hear my voice, and they follow me."*

Praying in His Will

"When you pray, go into your inner room, close your door and pray to your Father who is in secret, and your Father who sees what is done in secret will reward you.

Matthew 6:6

Spending time in a room alone with God in prayer will stretch your faith and sometimes change your attitude about the things you are praying for. If we pray in accordance with what His word says about prayer, we are praying in His will.

The Scripture says to "wait upon the Lord (and He) shall renew your strength" (Isaiah 40:31, NIV). Not only does that mean to not get ahead of the Lord, it can also mean to wait before Him in quietness until you get peace and direction.

Do not be too quick to end your prayers. Spend time listening too. Often in those quiet moments, you will not only feel His presence, you will receive direction, innovation, creativity, and answers to questions.

The Word of God teaches us many types of prayers. Here are a few:

Agreement Prayer - "Again I say to you, that if two of you agree on earth about anything that they may ask, it shall be done for them by my Father who is in heaven. For where two or three have gathered together in my name, I am in their midst" (Matthew 18: 19-20, NASB)

Thanksgiving Prayer - "Be earnest and unwearied and steadfast in your prayer (life), being (both) alert and intent in (your praying) with thanksgiving" (Colossians 4: 2)

Word Prayer - "For the Word of God is living and active. Sharper than any double-edged sword, it penetrates even to dividing soul and spirit, joints and marrow; it judges the thoughts and attitudes of the heart" (Hebrews 4: 12, NIV)

Warrior Prayer - "For the weapons of our warfare are not of the flesh, but divinely powerful for the destruction of fortresses" (2 Corinthians 10:4, NASB)

Workplace/Business Prayer - "I, therefore, the prisoner of the Lord, beseech you to walk worthy of the calling with which you were called, with all lowliness and gentleness, with longsuffering, bearing with one another in love; endeavoring to keep the unity of the Spirit in the bond of peace" (Ephesians 4:1-3, NKJV)

Wisdom Prayer - "If any of you is deficient in wisdom, let him ask of the giving God (Who gives) to every one liberally and ungrudgingly, without reproaching or faultfinding, and it will be given him" (James 1:5).

Guidance Prayer - "Commit your way to the Lord (roll and repose each care of your load on Him); trust (lean on, rely on, and be confident) also in Him and He will bring it to pass" (Psalm 37: 5)

Government Prayers – "If My people, which are called by My name, shall humble themselves, and pray, and seek My face, and turn from their wicked ways; then will I hear from Heaven, and will forgive their sin, and will heal their land" (2 Chronicles 7:14)

Do you need his strength today? Print this page. Get somewhere alone away from the hustle and bustle, and quietly read these prayers before the Lord making them personal. I'm agreeing with you.

Ready to Hear His Voice

Then Samuel answered, "Speak, Lord, for your servant is listening."
1 Samuel 3:10

When Moses replied to God in the burning bush, Moses was ready to hear God's voice. When Samuel heard God call his name he replied, "Here I am." Samuel was walking with the Lord when he was called: "So Samuel grew, and the Lord was with him" (1 Samuel 3:19, NKJV).

Henry Blackaby, author of, *Chosen to be God's Prophet: Lessons from the Life of Samuel,* writes, "God honors him who honors God by letting him hear His voice. When one - or a church - is not clearly hearing from God, it is because of sin."

In the times of Samuel and Eli (the priest), it was said, "The word of the Lord was RARE in those days; there was no widespread revelation" (1 Samuel 3:1, NKJV). Blackaby continues, "God honors the one who honors Him" (Blackaby).

And nothing honors God any more thoroughly than obedience!" Being ready to hear and obey God's voice means being prepared to do the smallest thing or the largest thing and trusting that it is all in God's plan.

One thing that can prevent us from hearing the voice of God and cause us to miss His plan is worry. On January 26, 2001, I wrote in my journal, "The Lord says, 'Be careful about one thing - your relationship to Me.'"

On that date, I had eight days to go to be reunited with my husband. In order to take the teaching career that God wanted me to take, I had to move from Washington State to Palm Desert, California. We were separated for eighteen months until my husband's retirement, visiting each other once every six weeks. It was one of the most challenging experiences of our marriage, but we were "ready" when He called us to the move, and we clearly heard His direction.

Now we needed to be ready for the task of starting a new life together. Our greatest concern was finances. The retirement pension would not be enough with my salary at the time.

God told me to keep my focus and trust on Him. I wrote in my journal, "This is the key to accomplishing the things God wants me to do. I must fellowship with Him more - not sharing negative worries, but sharing His Son, Jesus, who resides in me." I continued to practice the presence of God, rather than stress and worry, so that I would be open for His direction.

Our daughter and son-in-law had also moved to Palm Desert, so we were all together when Terry arrived. Our son-in-law worked at a resort hotel and mentioned that he had to go to his brother's wedding in Texas and did not know who would manage the hotel.

The Lord spoke to my heart quickly, "Suggest to Terry that he can do this job." I obeyed the voice and within a week Terry was trained in the reservation and guest check-in system, learning a new career.

When our son-in-law returned, the owner of the resort asked Terry to work in their golf pro shop. He never had to apply for a job after retiring to the desert and he's been at the resort ever since..

His willingness to serve opened the door to a new job that he enjoys. Instead of worry blocking the message, we were ready to hear God's voice, and He directed us.

Praying in the Spirit

Pray at all times (on every occasion, in every season) in the Spirit, with all (manner of) prayer and entreaty. To that end keep alert and watch with strong purpose and perseverance, interceding in behalf of all the saints.
                                                                        Ephesians 6:18

Prayer without the Holy Spirit's guidance becomes our willful prayers rather than God's will. If we get too sympathetic, we can pray for God to prevent something when God actually wants to allow the circumstance to happen.

For example, the toughest time I ever experienced praying God's will instead of my will was when my son's best friend was dying of stomach cancer at age 20 after serving in the Desert Storm War. He had spent a lot of time in our home, and we loved him as our own son.

I wanted to rush to the military hospital, lay hands on him and pray for his healing. I had the faith, and I had the compassion, but I did not yet have the mind of God. As time passed and I continued in prayer, it came clear to me that he was going to pass on, and what I needed to be in intercession for was his salvation.

He had been a pretty stubborn and rebellious young man for many years, and he was resisting spiritual counseling. As I stood in the gap for him in intercessory prayer, a friend of the family, a Lutheran pastor, was able to reach him, and in the end, he was able to accept Jesus Christ as his Savior before he died.

My son came to me two weeks before his friend's death and confessed through anguish and tears that he believed his friend was going to die. In that precious painful moment, the Holy Spirit was able to use me to comfort and prepare my son for the reality of the situation, rather than telling him to continue to have faith and to "not think such a negative thought."

Do not misunderstand. I am a woman of faith, and I will be the first one to agree in prayer with someone for healing when I sense in my spirit that God wants us to press in and fight. Yet I also know that God's ways are not our ways, and in the end He is more concerned with our spiritual souls than our physical victories.

Only God knows what it takes for each person to accept Jesus and have eternal life. Praying in the spirit is praying in God's will and focusing on God's interests and concerns in others' lives.

Receiving Direction From God

Delight yourself also in the Lord, and HE will give you the desires and secret petitions of your heart. Commit your way to the Lord... trust... also in Him and He will bring it to pass.

Psalm 37:4-5

Many Christians ask me how to know God's will and direction for their lives. I always reply that if Christ lives in you, then your heart's desire is from God.

In fact, when God says He wants to give us our heart's desires, He put those desires in our hearts! We think we are making these ideas up, but He actually placed them there.

In other words, His will becomes our will. Of course, in balance, any fleshly desire that rises itself up against the Word of God is not of God.

Sometimes we make decisions to the best of our ability, responding to information and circumstances that come across our paths. My advice is, if you cannot get a confirmation of what to do, then you have two choices: 1) Wait and do nothing, and God will be faithful to stir your spirit in that direction in a stronger way; or 2) Take one step in that direction, and God will be faithful to take away your peace of heart and mind, and you will know to back the truck up!

Are you feeling restless? Seeking new opportunities, but not sure? Confused about where you are now?

Always go back to the last direction God gave you, reflect on that, make sure you have done everything He asked you do, and keep being faithful there until He opens the next door. If you are exploring your options, keep exploring. That desire to explore is from Him, if only to discover that where you are now is the best thing possible for the time being.

In 2005, my husband and I explored our options to retire in Tucson, Arizona ten years from the date we visited. We heard that there were great deals for housing and that the time to buy was immediate, because everything was going up rapidly. We imagined Tucson to be a small western town with quaint shopping streets and large homes for low prices.

We took a trip there and discovered just the opposite. The area has 800,000 people and is growing, rush hour traffic, a poorly planned city, and over-priced homes. The backyards are mostly all gravel and cacti with very few trees. It was not anything we imagined and for now have decided we are in the best place possible for retirement.

Were we out of God's will to even go exploring? Absolutely not! God knew that in order for us to make a natural choice in accordance with His will, we needed to do some analytical evaluation, and He provided a natural way for us to do that. The trip gave us great contentment with our present circumstances.

If God called us to Tucson, of course, we would obey. However, I believe it would be rare for God to make us do something we are not comfortable with.

Laurie Beth Jones, author of the national bestseller, *The Path: Creating Your Mission Statement for Work and for Life,* tells her readers to be careful of the false assumption, belief or fear that God's will is to have you do something you do not like or are not good at, so that, through the suffering that results, you will become humble. She writes, "Beware of taking on missions that fit someone else's needs – but not your particular interests of gifts."

Finally, if you need an answer, God will give you one, " If any of you lacks wisdom, he should ask God, who gives generously to all without finding fault, and it will be given to him. But when he asks, he must believe and not doubt, because he who doubts is like a wave of the sea, blown and tossed by the wind." (James 1: 5-6, NIV).

Doing the Last Thing He Told You

Behold, we are going up to Jerusalem.

Luke 18:31 NKJV

Jesus knew that his life was in danger in Jerusalem, yet he kept heading in that direction. A few years ago, a sister-in-the-Lord wrote me a note that said, "If you are not getting any direction from the Lord as to what to do next, then just do the last thing He told you to do."

I often find myself at a crossroads in life, at the end of one experience and waiting for the next, discouraged at the lack of ministry activity and desiring to reach a higher, more meaningful purpose for my life. Jesus never hurried through bad times, and He never lingered in blessed times – He just kept walking toward His destiny one day at a time.

Hebrews 4:1 reminds us, "Therefore, since the promise of entering His rest still stands, let us be careful that none of you be found to have fallen short of it" (NIV). The Christian REST is being fully surrendered to the Lordship of Christ and the Holy Spirit and trusting that God will do the things that He said He will do in our lives.

If God's Word says, "I know the thoughts and plans I have for you…plans to prosper you and not to harm you, plans to give you hope and a future" (Jeremiah 29:11, NIV), then God's Word is TRUE.

Begin praising God today for His final outcome in your life. Be content and at rest in the last thing He told you to do, and trust that He will open the next door for you in His time.

Ultimately the pressures and the waiting are making us more Christ-like for our final destiny – Heaven! God has a perfect plan for you! Be blessed today.

Trust in the Wilderness

(We are) selected and called to be saints (God's people), together with all those who in any place call upon and give honor to the name of our Lord Jesus Christ, both their Lord and ours.

1 Corinthians 1:2

We are so enthusiastic when God gives us a vision or gives us a glimpse of our purpose, but we sometimes recoil at the character building preparation it takes to get us there.

In the 35 years I have served the Lord, I can truly say that it is the tough circumstances that made me who I am today, not the positive happy ones. Why? Because my faith, love, joy, peace, and my ability to forgive others, grew in the midst of the fire and the flood.

I recall one particular day when I did not think I could go forward with the vision God had for my life. Under God's direction, I made a decision to run for school board, and the local press daily reported on me as a Christian candidate, creating false fears of what that meant in the public schools.

The teachers in that district were cruel to my children and incited the other children against them. One day my teenage son came home from high school and said, "I hate you for running for school board. I will never forgive you for taking away a normal high school experience from me. Everyone is mocking me."

I sobbed on my bed that day and said, "God, how can this be of you? How can you call this mother to take a stand for the children of this district and lose my own child? This cannot be of you."

In that moment of anguish, the Lord spoke to my heart and said, "I have a plan for your children too. In the years ahead, they are going to have to face a greater persecution than this as the hatred toward Christians increases on this earth. There will be a time that it will be far more difficult to stand for your beliefs. In my LOVE for your children, I must prepare them for the calling I have on their lives, and I am preparing you to trust me completely. Be at peace. It's going to be all right."

Two years later at graduation, in front of 3,000 parents and students (and my family), I was introduced as President of the School Board. The teachers had instigated the students to "boo" me when I stood on the stage.

It was arranged for me to give my son his diploma, but I knew he would be too humiliated to acknowledge me as his mother. I was prepared for my son to grab his diploma and run, and I would not blame him. But instead, in front of all those people, my son hugged me and whispered in my ear, "I love you, mom." I shed tears of joy because God had completed His perfect plan, and my son was going to be "all right."

The Mind of God

I am the Bread of Life. He who comes to Me will never be hungry, and he who believes in and cleaves to and trusts in and relies on Me will never thirst any more (at any time).

John 6:34-35

Without the mind of God, we will not only be unclear about God's will for our lives, we will involve ourselves in things that could eventual cause burn out or even rob us of our finances. Repeatedly, I have people approach me for money on the street. My good heart wants to give to anyone in need, but the person asking may have evil intent for the money (i.e. drugs), and my giving would be enabling, rather than doing the work of the Lord.

I have to pray to get the mind of God in these situations, or be a good steward of my money by only buying gasoline or food. One of my favorite songs says, "I would that all would be fed and live in divine health. But don't you know their soul has to be made whole first of all, or they never will know Me."

The ultimate objective of God is to guide people to Jesus, so that they can know the Father. The disciples said to the beggar, "We have no money for you, but we have something greater – the good news of Jesus Christ who can make you whole."

Having the mind of God is as simple as being tuned in to the inner feelings and directions you get. The more you practice using your radar and following through, the clearer the messages of God will become.

For example, in 2005, I sat in the airport waiting for a flight. I saw a young man dressed like a cowboy sitting by himself (he was only 15 years old). I did not hear the Lord say "walk over and visit him." Rather, I felt this strong push in my soul to go sit near him and start up a conversation.

I followed that feeling and discovered a very scared young man whose father, a Marine, had just got shipped to Iraq. He was having trouble in the high school in California, so he was leaving his mother and brothers and sisters to go live with his grandparents in Texas to complete school.

It was in his sharing that I began to hear the mind of God and minister to this young man. I assured him that God was with him, that his father was going to be all right, and that he was doing the right thing. I told him that God had a great purpose for his life, and he needed to get back into church with his grandparents and seek the Lord.

By the time he got on the plane, his spirit was at peace, and his face showed it. With tears in his eyes, you could tell he knew God had just touched his heart.

The Witness of the Spirit

The Spirit Himself bears witness with our spirit...

Romans 8:16 NKJV

There are so many Christian words and phrases that I learned over the years that young people or new believers have never heard of. Generations of Christians raised their children in structured churches where these terms were frequently used.

Today, family church attendance is low, and the religious terminology has faded out of everyday language. My pastor tells me that when I use those "old" phrases, I should make it a "teaching moment" and explain to newer believers what I am talking about.

One of those phrases is "getting a witness of the spirit." When people receive Jesus as their Savior, they often receive a sense of peace, forgiveness, or a "knowing" in their spirit. It is this witness of the Spirit of God that confirms to them that what just happened was very real. It is the Spirit of God within us, the Holy Spirit, who Jesus sent to reside in us, who bears witness to truth.

When we are receiving a message from God through another person, receiving a personal revelation in our spirit directly from Him, walking in obedience according to His Word, or following the path he told us to walk, we sense a confirmation that what we are doing or what we are hearing is of Him. It is a knowing in the "knower" of our soul.

If someone is telling you something in a mean ugly manner, you know it is not of the Spirit. If someone is telling you something in love, a truth you need to hear, and you feel God's presence in the message, even if it hurts, it is from God.

We spend so much time trying to not hear what the Lord is telling us because we are afraid that His direction will require too much of us, or we prefer to follow our own evil ways. Whatever the argument you give God or have with yourself, it keeps you from the most glorious experiences with God on earth. When we finally yield, all heaven breaks forth upon us.

In the *Chronicles of Narnia* by C.S. Lewis, Aslan is the Lion of Narnia and is seen in the allegory as King Jesus, Lord of Heaven and Earth.

When two children, referred to as "sons of Adam" enter into Narnia, they can see all the beauty and can hear all the beasts talk.

When the children's uncle, who is unkind and also a practitioner of white magic, accidentally enters Narnia, he is afraid of everything and can hear nothing. As a result, he is tormented.

The children want to know if Aslan (Jesus) can do anything to "unfrighten" him. Aslan replies, "I wish I could help this sinner, but I cannot comfort him for he has made himself unable to hear my voice. If I spoke to him, he would only hear grumblings and roarings."

Aslan goes on to say, "Oh, Adam's sons, how cleverly you defend yourselves against all that might do you good! I will give him the only gift he is still able to receive." Aslan then puts a sleep upon the old man and removes him from his torment.

We must not harden our hearts to the messages the Spirit is trying to bear witness to. Jesus said, "The work of God is this: to believe in the One He has sent" (John 6:29, NIV).

The Reason for WAIT

Peter said to Him, "Lord, why can I not follow You now? I will lay down my life for Your sake."

John 13:37 NKJV

"Wait" was the first lesson God taught me over 30 years ago – and I am still learning it! I would get a glimpse of what He wanted to do through me and rush off in that direction, acting on impulse. I caused so much heartache and experienced great disappointment, because I did not wait on God's timing.

When God tells us to "wait," or there is a silence from heaven and we are forced to wait, we must be careful to not fill that space with busyness. God gave me the picture of a straight path representing His direction for my life. He showed me that every time I stepped off the path, not waiting on His direction, I looped up, around and came back to the exact same spot on the path. I realized that some of my loops ranged from two weeks to two years!

Our God is so patient, He waits for us to expire ourselves in our free will until we once again come to Him for direction. I decided that a much faster way to get to my destiny was to wait. I discovered that God knew what I was ready for and when, and the waiting process was preparing me and disciplining me so that the enemy would not defeat me.

Peter wanted to follow Jesus now, not knowing that it led to crucifixion and death on the cross. He went from saying he would lay his life down for God to denying Jesus three times. Jesus knew Peter and predicted the outcome.

In January of 1984, I was director of a successful church pre-school and daycare center, and I was very busy with Girl Scouts, Red Cross and church activities. God spoke to my heart with this message: "I want you to give everything up, study your Bible every day for a year, continue to pray for your children and the public schools, and wait on Me."

It took a few months, but I eventually let go of everything, found a director for the daycare, and came home. About three months after the one-year timeframe, I thought God had forgotten me. I felt my life was "nothing," and I was sure I had missed the mark.

A friend came into my life just when I needed it and said, "This waiting is the most powerful thing you can do for God. It will break the back of Satan and give you supernatural strength. Waiting on God IS a ministry. Do not give up."

That summer, the Lord called me to my assignment – I was to run for school board and take a very controversial stand for moral values in our public schools. For over a year, He had prepared me with studies of great leaders of the Bible who He had also called into public ministry.

The school board election victory took me rapidly into a nation-wide ministry of teaching other parents how to pray for their children and how to make a difference in their schools. By 1988, just four years after the call "to wait," I had traveled to forty-four states with God's message.

The "wait" in His Word and in prayer prepared me for something I could not have imagined. God knows what your future holds and what you can handle – trust Him.

The Voice of God

I heard the voice of the Lord, saying, "Whom shall I send? And who will go for Us?"

Isaiah 6:8

I am of the opinion that God is transmitting messages to us all the time, but we are too busy or our minds are too noisy for us to hear. Hannah Hurnard, author of *God's Transmitters,* writes, "Prayer is essentially the contact of our minds with the mind of God, resulting in a real conversation with Him."

The Lord tells us in Scripture to have our minds stayed upon Him. The Word of God is also a vehicle of God's communication, but without allowing the Holy Spirit in our hearts to teach us, we are deaf to what the Spirit of God is saying.

Many Christians ask me how I know it is God speaking to me. More than a voice, it is a thought, and the thought comes with the presence of God in the form of peace or a deep stillness.

When we know the Lord and spend time with Him and in His Word, the Bible promises that His sheep will know His voice. At times, if there are clear words, it comes from my spirit, not from my head. The Holy Spirit communicates to my spirit, and my spirit communicates to my brain in the English language.

Most importantly, I do not seek the voice. I seek God. We can trust that if we acknowledge God, He will direct our paths (Proverbs 3:6). If our expectation is in God to direct us, then we can trust that He will.

My first experience with hearing God's voice was when I was in high school. I was not yet a believer in Jesus, and I did not have a clear understanding of God. One evening, I got locked in the stairwell of the high school on the night of a snow blizzard.

I had arrived early for drill team and sought a place of protection in the storm. The inside doors automatically locked when I pulled them shut behind me, and the outside doors in the stairwell were chained. I soon realized that no one was coming to drill.

The lights went out in the main school area, and I suddenly realized that the janitor had shut the building down. I panicked and shook every door leading to the hallway on three stories, but nothing budged. I sat on the bottom stair and began to cry with fear and anxiety. Suddenly, I heard a soothing voice within me say, "Be quiet." I stopped for a second and then started to cry again.

The voice within was louder, "Be quiet and listen!" I froze. I then heard the door latch click. The voice said, "Go open it." I walked over, and the door opened. I walked home in the snowstorm with tears on my cheeks somehow knowing I had an encounter with God, and I sealed the experience in my heart. It was that encounter (probably my guardian angel) that caused me to continue to seek Him until He found me.

Messengers of the Lord

These things I have spoken to you, that My joy may remain in you, and that your joy may be full.

John 15:11

The world promotes the concept that living a full and life is based on circumstances, but a satisfying life really lies in fellowship and oneness with God – the same oneness that Jesus enjoyed. In fact, too much thought about our circumstances and the cares of the world will rob our joy. The cares of the world and the occupation of taking care of material things can block the presence and voice of God in our lives. When we are focused on the cares of the world, we are focused more on ourselves than on others.

The Israelites were set free from Babylon and led back to Jerusalem in 538 B.C. They departed in three groups with about 80 years in between each group. Children were being born in captivity while their freedom was taking place. A priest named Ezra led out the second of the three groups. While traveling back to God's "land," Ezra had to call the people into repentance because they had adopted all the world practices of the Babylonians.

There were generations who did not even know the word or the commandments of the Lord. I believe this is the state of our nation today. We have adopted so many of the world's practices, we now think they are normal. The children of America are getting further and further away from the Lord and yet, they are unhappier. Nothing seems to satisfy this generation. The covetousness of our hearts has separated us from the voice of God.

God is raising up some Ezra's today. God's voice wants to be heard in the churches, heard in the land, and heard in the workplace. God wants His people to be set apart from the world and to have a sweet fragrance that others notice.

The Bible is an instruction book for believers, not for unbelievers. The message of "setting ourselves apart" is for the followers of God – not the followers of the world's standards. Most "Ezra's" (priests, preachers, teachers, and prophets) will be speaking to the churches to get ready, get aligned with God's standards, and get into His presence. Other "Daniel's" and "Esther's" will be setting an example of light and wisdom in a world of darkness. Some "Apostle Paul's" will be bold evangelists. And many "Nehemiah's" will be building and leading the churches to prepare for the great harvest.

These messengers and messages of God are to bring us joy – not resentment. We are to be joyful that God is raising up leaders to guide us and direct us. Be aware of what God is saying to His people.

I heard a great quote that may apply to many of you who are reading this: "A true leader turns his back to his followers." A true leader cannot be concerned with the whining and complaining, the persecution, or people caught up in what the world thinks is "politically correct." A true leader must follow God and trust that those that are called by Him will follow the messenger of God.

Are You A Friend of Jesus?

I have called you my friends...

John 15:15

God wants me to be His friend. I am trying to understand what that means.

Bruce Wilkinson says in *Secrets of the Vine,* "Unless your friendship with God becomes your first priority, you will never fulfill your true destiny as a Christian or a leader." Moses was a friend to God and had daily conversations with Him. "And the Lord spoke to Moses face to face, as a man speaks to his friend" (Exodus 33: 11).

Deuteronomy 13:6, describes a friend as someone who "is as your own soul." James 2:23 says, "Abraham believed God...and he was called God's friend."

To be God's friend is to believe what God tells you and to receive His gifts and blessings. God said Israel, "Fear not; for I AM with thee: be not dismayed; for I AM thy God: I will strengthen thee; yea, I will help thee; yea, I will uphold thee with the right hand of my righteousness" (Isaiah 41:10, KJV). Now that's a friend!

"A friend loves at all times" (Proverbs 17:17). That means God loves me, and I love him no matter what.

Jesus had a few things to say about friendship too. He said, "Greater hath no man than this, that a man lay down his life for his friends" (John 15:13, KJV).

He also said, "You are my friends, if you do what command" (v. 14, NIV). He continues in verse 15: "I have called you friends, for everything that I learned from my Father I have made known to you."

In September 2001, I wrote in my journal:

> *You, Lord, have been my Father and my Brother, and I have even depended on You at times to be my Husband. Without a godly example of a father or brother, I have struggled with this definition of our relationship. Now I am grown spiritually, and I want to be your Friend as You are mine. I know what that looks like from*

reading your Scriptures, and I want to be the best friend possible. As my confidence in our friendship grows, I know I can let you be a friend through me to others without expecting anything in return.

There is an old religious song, "What a Friend We Have in Jesus." We casually say, "Jesus wants to be your friend." Too frequently, we forget that Jesus wants us to be His friend too. The Bible says the best way to do that is to follow His teachings on love.

Part 5

Keys to Success

The Anchor Holds

(Now) we have this (hope) as a sure and steadfast anchor of the soul (it cannot slip and it cannot break down under whoever steps out upon it—a hope)...

Hebrews 6:19

In third world countries, people are looking for a daily meal. In America, we are all looking for success.

We seem to lose sight of God's true purpose for our life. In the marketing campaigns "achieving higher success" is a powerful sales tool.

Sometimes God's purpose may be the exact opposite of success when He is building strength and character in our life. When we are given a dream or a vision, we believe that God's purpose for us is to get us to the end goal where we can announce our success. However, God's purpose may be the journey, not the final destination.

God's purpose for us is to depend on Him and on His power and to stretch our faith in new dimensions.

In Mark 6, the disciples found themselves in a storm in the dark at about 3:00 a.m. in the morning, and the Scripture says they were troubled and tormented. Jesus walked on the sea and came to them and found them screaming, agitated, and full of fear.

He said to them, "Take heart! I AM! Stop being alarmed and afraid!" (Mark 6:50). And the storm ceased as He entered the boat. There was no land in sight; there was no clear goal in that moment, and they did not know what awaited them on the other side.

What they did know was the absolute certainty that everything was all right, because they saw Him walking on the sea. They fully understood the "I AM" of God and all that He is and ceased to fear.

Lawrence Chewning and Ray Boltz wrote the song, *The Anchor Holds:*

> *"I have journeyed through the long dark night out on the open sea*
> *by faith alone, sight unknown, and yet, His eyes were watching me.*
> *The anchor holds though the ship is battered, the anchor holds*
> *though the sails are torn. I have fallen on my knees, as I faced the*

raging seas, the anchor hold, in spite of the storm. I've had visions, and I've had dreams, I've even held them in my hands. But I never knew, that they could slip right through like they were only grains of sand. Now I have been young, and I am older now and there has been beauty these eyes have seen. But it was in the night I faced the storms in my life, that's where God proved His love to me."

The real goal is to see what we do in a storm. Success in God's eyes is our ability to stay calm, faithful and unconfused in the midst of the turmoil of life.

The real goal is our ability to hang onto the anchor in the midst of a storm. Now that's success!

Spiritual Darkness

If anyone is willing to do His will, he will know of the teaching, whether it is of God or whether I speak for myself.

John 7:17 NASB

Jesus gives instruction to not come to the altar if your brother has something against you, but to go immediately to your brother and be reconciled. How many of us hear that prompting of the Holy Spirit, but hesitate and delay? If we are not growing spiritually, there may be something we need to examine and bring into the light.

Whenever Jesus spoke the truth regarding the spiritual darkness of the religious leaders, they sought to kill Him. Their hearts were not open to His truth.

Is their anything you are avoiding in your discussions with Jesus because you do not intend to obey? Is there someone He wants you to forgive? Is there financial giving you have refused participate in? Is there a principle in His Word that He wants you to be open to?

If you are resisting or avoiding, it may be the exact place you need to walk toward. If you do not, you will be spiritually stuck.

In the marketplace, we are also in a hurry to evade difficult and uncomfortable situations. There is often an opportunity for growth if we push on through, leaning on Him for strength and wisdom.

Keep in mind that sometimes it is not the circumstances He wants to change, it is our hearts He wants to enlighten. Before you seek new direction, always clear up matters of the heart first.

The good news is, God wants to bring light into our darkness: "Call to Me and I will answer you and show you great and mighty things, fenced in and hidden, which you do not know (do not distinguish and recognize, have knowledge of and understand)" (Jeremiah 33:3).

If you are in a spiritually dark time, invite God to illuminate your heart and mind and be open to what He is teaching you.

What's in Your Heart?

But the things that proceed out of the mouth come from the heart...
Matthew 15:18 NASB

There is a credit card commercial, which asks, "What's in your wallet?" Jesus came to the earth and asked the uncomfortable question to those who thought they were righteous, "What's in your heart?" Here lies the great stumbling block of all time.

When my daughter was a pre-teen, she was in the car with friends who were of a religion that believed in works not grace. They passed a billboard near Seattle, Washington and read, "Believe on the Lord Jesus Christ, and you shall be saved."

The mother said, "Isn't it sad that they think that is all there is to it?"

The big deception of Satan is for people to believe that we are saved by works and not by grace. Jesus makes clear that "being good" is not enough. What He wants is for us to allow Him to examine our hearts and expose anything in motive or attitude, thought or feeling that would eventually manifest itself in sin.

It is difficult for many people, including Christians, to believe that they could ever commit the crimes of those in prison. We are always so quick to judge, not realizing that we all have the same evil potential.

"For out of the heart proceed evil thoughts, murders, adulteries, fornications, thefts, false witness, blasphemies: these are the things which defile a man..." (Matthew 15:19-20).

Jesus made it clear in this passage of Scripture that He views our evil thoughts as equal to the sins of a criminal. He warns us that we all have the potential for evil if we do not yield our hearts to Him.

I apply this same concept in my marketplace calling. No matter how much skill I attain or education I receive, it is only by the grace of God that I can be successful.

We usually come to God in our inadequacies, asking Him to give us the ability and wisdom we need. I am now learning to humble myself before Him even when things are going well.

When we start the day in prayer recognizing our need for God, the Holy Spirit can reveal anything that needs to be cleansed and protect us from the subtle pride that tries to infiltrate our thinking. We all have natural gifts and talents that we give back to the world, but I prefer to give them back to God first, and let Him decide each day how they will be used.

We must not use the world's unit of measurement regarding our goodness; we must use the Lord's standards. When we use His measuring stick, we quickly recognize that we cannot measure up and that only by forgiveness and the grace of God through the redemption of Jesus Christ can we be called a child of God.

The Scripture makes it clear that everything we have is through Jesus Christ: "But it is from Him that you have your life in Christ Jesus, Whom God made our Wisdom from God…" (1 Corinthians 1:30).

According to this Scripture, if you need wisdom, it is already yours THOUGH CHRIST.

Be Quick to Forgive

For if you forgive people their trespasses (their reckless and willful sins, leaving them, letting them go and giving up resentment), your heavenly Father will also forgive you.

Matthew 6: 14

Too many people take resentment to the very gates of death thinking they can take their stubbornness and anger with them.

I had a very close friend who died of cancer. She had been in a verbally abusive and extremely controlling marriage for 40 years. Her husband never let her get a driver's license and controlled every aspect of her life.

I was one of the few people he trusted, so I had permission to take her shopping and to Bible study. Toward the end of her illness, my husband and I welcomed her and her fifteen-year old pregnant daughter into our home because she feared her husband's physical abuse against both of them, especially because of her daughter's condition.

My friend died ten days before the birth of her granddaughter. The day before she died in the hospital, I had arrived about fifteen minutes after her husband had visited her.

I found her full of anger and expressing her hatred toward this man. Even in the end, he was "yanking her chain" and making threats about their daughter and the baby-to-be.

I took her hand and said, "My friend, you are about to enter the kingdom of heaven into the presence of Jesus Christ Our Lord. You cannot take this anger with you. You must forgive him once and for all before you die. God will deal with your husband, and I will watch over your daughter and grandchild. You need to focus on the peace and forgiveness of the Lord."

She confessed her sin and was immediately full of peace. The next night at midnight another sister-in-the-Lord and I went to the hospital and sang Christian songs at her bedside, holding her hands, as she passed over into eternity completely free.

Is there unforgiveness in your heart? It may be preventing you from going the next step in God's plan for your life. Let it go.

Zero Tolerance Policy

For it is written: "Be holy, because I am holy."

1 Peter 1:16 NIV

Holiness is a tough concept, because it makes us so uncomfortable. It seems like something we cannot attain, when in reality it is not about us, but about the work of God we are allowing in our lives. It is about giving God the go ahead to finish what He began.

Holiness means to take every thought and action captive into the will of God; it is moving toward a "zero tolerance" policy for sin in your life. For example, using profanity because everyone else is doing it is not acceptable.

2 Timothy 3:2 says that in the last days "people will be lovers of self (utterly) self-centered, lovers of money and aroused by an inordinate (greedy) desire for wealth, proud and arrogant and contemptuous boasters. They will be abusive (blasphemous, scoffing), disobedient to parents, ungrateful, unholy and profane." Verse 4 says "(they will be) lovers of sensual pleasures and vain amusements more than and rather than lovers of God."

If we begin to even practice in a small way ungratefulness, arrogance, greed, or profaneness, we need to cast it out of our lives in Jesus' name.

I heard a preacher say this week, "I kept asking God over and over for forgiveness, but I kept making the same mistakes. God told me, 'I've already forgiven you – that's done. You need to call these things out and pray your victory!"

What does that look like? Here is an example of prayer to deal with discontentment that will eventually lead to greed, love of money, depression, and a spirit of worldliness:

> *Lord, I thank you for everything you have given me. According to Matthew 18:18, I bind the spirit of discontentment in my life in Jesus' Name and according to Jude 9, I say 'Lord, rebuke it.' I release a spirit of thankfulness and praise into my life, and I ask you Holy Spirit to help me focus on whatever is good, lovely, and of good report. I am grateful for your love, I am grateful for your son*

Jesus in my life, and I am grateful for a promised home in heaven. Forgive me my ungratefulness and release me from that bondage now in Jesus' name, Amen.

Praying God's Word in your life is walking toward holiness. It is allowing God to do His perfect work in you. Pretty soon, your behaviors will start aligning with your prayers. Take every negative thought and action captive into the Word of God.

Have you been slipping? Then start today with your zero-tolerance policy, and do not forget to ask God to help you.

The Greatest Temptation

No temptation has overtaken you except such as is common to man...
1Corinthians 10:13 NKJV

What does the devil hate the most? Your prayers!

He will tempt you to put prayer at the bottom of the priority list. If that doesn't work, and you are an effective prayer warrior, he will tempt you to take the glory for your prayers, instead of giving God the glory.

In other words, temptation comes to us in accordance with the level where we are. In our early walk with the Lord, it may come to us at in the form of lust, greed, dishonesty, or resentment. Later, it can come with the temptation of taking short cuts against God's will or spiritual pride in our Christian successes.

K.P. Yohannan, author of *Reflecting His Image,* was born and raised in India and is the founder and international director of Gospel for Asia. He has written more than 175 books and lives near Dallas with his wife.

Yohannan writes that the devil hates prayer more than choir practice, seminars, conferences, and Christian concerts; and he will do everything in his power to stop us from engaging in this dangerous activity. "In fact, prayer is so destructive to him that he is more than happy to see us choose instead to listen to a sermon, read a Christian book, or work for charity."

If the devil cannot stop us from praying, then he will tempt us into believing that all the great victories in our lives happened because of our prayers or because of our intercession, or because we knew how to defeat the devil. "When things are happening, the enemy tempts us to trust in our prayer activity, our expertise on spiritual warfare, our elite group, and our dynamite church leadership" (Yohannan).

How do we avoid the temptation to take glory away from God when we are serving Him? Yohannan concludes with this message, "Examine our hearts daily to see if we are placing our confidence in anything other than Jesus alone. God seeks followers and intercessors who believe with all their hearts that it is 'not by might, nor by power, but by My Spirit, says the Lord of hosts'" (Zechariah 4:6).

A few minutes of prayer with total dependence on the Lord is worth more than days of weeping in our own strength. We may cry out all day long and see nothing happen, yet when Elijah prayed a few words, and fire came down from heaven!

Since temptation is not something we can escape from, it is a good thing to be aware that the enemy is designing some subtle plan to bring you into a trap that you are not aware of. That is why Jesus taught us to pray, "Deliver us from temptation." "Submit therefore to God. Resist the devil and he will flee from you" (James 4:7, NASB).

Above all else, remain humble and keep praying.

Beware the Little Foxes

Take us the foxes, the little foxes that spoil the vines: for our vines have tender grapes.

Song of Solomon 2:15 KJV

When we have experienced victory, we think it is the least likely time we will stumble and fall. Trying to predict where the temptation will come, or in what area we may trip up is dangerous. If we are not on guard at all times, we will find that it is often that which we least expect that proves too dangerous.

The ocean may look safe, but underneath in the undercurrent, the enemy is planning a way to pull you down. We must stay alert and remain under the protective shadow of His wings.

I recall when I had an intense week with a heavy schedule. I was giving presentations at 7:00 a.m. and teaching as late as 10:00 p.m. I tried not to focus on the things that could have overwhelmed me, and I practiced all week walking in the presence of God, leaning on Him for strength and wisdom.

On Friday afternoon, after an 8-hour training session, I drove home and thanked God for the victory of getting through the week. I was feeling very pleased and enjoying a sense of victory. Within one hour of the victory, a person made a false accusation based on misinformation, and I walked right into a trap of pain and drain in the sanctuary of my own home.

A prayer covering at the end of my week might have prevented the little "fox" that tried to spoil the victory and our relationship.

We would like to think that Satan would eventually give up and grow weary of seeking to defeat and discourage us, but he will not. Satan is always planning a trap for us, and it is the "little foxes" that that we cannot see that trip us.

But there is a way to stay alert and remain protected from his deceitful assignments. When we have a great victory and are walking in spiritual success, we can come to our Good Shepherd in love, worship, and prayer.

When Daniel was given the interpretation of the King's dream and his life was spared, he cried out, "Blessed be the name of God forever and ever! For wisdom and might are his...I thank You and praise You, O God of my fathers, Who has given me wisdom and might and has made known to me what we desired of You" (Daniel 2:20-23).

We must also beseech the Father as Jesus did in the Lord's Prayer when he prayed, "Keep us from temptation and deliver us from evil."

The good news is, even when the enemy tries to defeat us, God will take what was meant for evil and turn it into good. "God is our refuge and strength, a very present help in trouble" (Psalm 46:1, NASB).

Confession Versus Rationalization

He is faithful and just to forgive our sins, and to cleanse us from all unrighteousness.

1 John 1: 9 KJV

Have you ever heard the phrase "carnal Christian?" It means Christians walking according to the flesh instead of according to the Spirit.

A Christian that gossips, is jealous, causes strife, or constantly complains is a carnal Christian. Apostle Paul recognized this as a common problem when he wrote specific messages about it to the churches in Rome, Corinth, Ephesus, and Galatia.

Over 2,000 years later, pastors are still preaching the same message - to let your actions speak louder than your words. All of us have the potential of being carnal; the question is, do we ignore carnality, make excuses for it, and rationalize it away? Or do we confess it?

A friend of mine was a state highway patrolman for over 20 years. He told me that most people who are pulled over for speeding or other infractions have excuses for their behavior.

He heard many creative stories over the years. He shared that when someone finally admitted they were wrong and gave no excuse, it was so refreshing to hear the truth, that he did not give them a ticket. He commented that it amazed him that grown adults still behave as children and will not face honestly the consequences of their actions.

I think God looks at His children the same way, and He is tired of the excuses or insincere confessions.

One night I was driving back home late at night from my university teaching assignment. It was close to midnight, and I was very tired. I came to an intersection with no traffic except for one vehicle behind me.

I suddenly realized I was in the wrong lane (the road ahead was washed out from floods), and I changed lanes and turned left. The lane I was first in was green, but the left turn lane had a red arrow, and in my confusion and tiredness, I went through it.

185

The one vehicle behind me was a police officer, and I was pulled over. I was so embarrassed and discouraged. I told him I was tired and forgot about the road being washed out and failed to get in the left turn lane. But I also confessed that I was wrong, I made a mistake, and I apologized for my actions.

He went back to his car to check my license. I put my head down on the steering wheel and simply said, "God, I could use a little grace right now."

The officer came back and told me to be more careful in the future and let me go. He knew I was a professor and added with a smile, "I just hope you are not teaching law enforcement!"

The point is we will make mistakes because we are human, but "If we freely admit that we have sinned and confess out sins. He is faithful and just (true to His own nature and promises) and will forgive our sins (dismiss our lawlessness) and continuously cleanse us from all unrighteousness (everything not in conformity to His will in purpose, thought, and action" (1 John 1: 9).

Conditioning Our Spirit

I have many more things to say to you, but you cannot bear them now.
John 16:12 NASB

Conditioning our spirit is just as important as conditioning our body. If we do not exercise our faith in the small things, we will not be ready for the big challenges.

If we do not develop our spirits, we will not be prepared for a higher revelation from God. Just as we physically start out as babies, so we spiritually start out needing "milk" not "meat" when we become born again.

Perhaps you have tried to be disciplined in your devotion time, but it has become a ritual with no revelation or meaning. Abiding in the Word does strengthen our spirits, but I think the reason God wants us to study the Word is to discover through the stories how He takes care of His children in difficult times.

Baby Christians whine and cry because they have not studied the Word to see how the story turns out in the end and how God is always faithful. Baby Christians struggle with the reality that bad things do happen to good people, and life can be unfair.

Mature Christians know that God is working in their midst even when He seems absent. Laurie Beth Jones in *Jesus CEO* writes "Jesus saw love in control of the plan." When Pilate threw Jesus into prison, Jesus said, "You would have no authority over me if it were not given to you from on high."

David turned down opportunities to kill Saul, because He knew he was God's anointed. Even though it did not make sense, he had to trust that God knew what was best to develop his character and prepare him to be King.

Joseph is my favorite story. He was an innocent man thrown into slavery and prison, and yet he is later made second-in-command to the Pharaoh.

Many Christians are still "babies" even though they have walked with the Lord for many years. Hebrews 5:12-14 states: "For though by this time you ought to be teachers, you have need again for someone to teach the elementary principles of the oracles of God, and you have come to need milk and not solid food. For everyone who partakes only of milk is not accustomed to the word of righteousness, for he is an infant. But solid food belongs to those who are of full age, that is, those who by reason of use have their senses exercised to discern both good and evil" (NASB).

ABOVE ALL ELSE, seek His Wisdom, read His Word. There is no better time than now to GROW and condition your spirit!

Just Add Water

But his delight and desire are in the law of the Lord, and on His law (the precepts, the instructions, the teachings of God) he habitually meditates (ponders and studies) by day and by night

Psalm 1: 2

If you take a glass with a small amount of grape juice in the bottom and begin to add water to it, at first, it will be diluted, but still appears purple. If you continue to pour water into the glass, it will eventually displace the grape juice and the entire glass will be full of clear water.

This is how holiness in our life takes place. Rather than trying through works to get rid of the flesh and sin in our life, we only need to continue to fill our vessel with the Word of God and allow the Holy Spirit to displace everything that is not of God.

Most of us avoid a disciplined life. We avoid regular exercise, eating the right food, and the routine of reading God's Word.

Yet we all recall being taught by our parents to get our homework done immediately after school so that we could play the rest of the evening. It is called "delayed gratification." In our spiritual walk, our first priority should be to allow the Holy Spirit to fill us through prayer and the Word of God, then our days will go much better.

If you are an extremely busy person, as I am, place the Word of God in various places in your home, car, and work. A few Scripture cards in your desk drawer, a booklet of Scripture promises in your glove compartment, and faith-strengthening Scriptures on your mirror or refrigerator can give you the drink of water you need in a dry time throughout the day.

One Minute Prayers

"Whatever you ask in My name, that I will do."
John 14:13 NASB

There is a famous management book by Ken Blanchard titled, *The One Minute Manager.* It talks about how research of employees revealed that people just want their managers to occasionally spend a minute with them to give them a positive word about how they are doing on the job.

Blanchard discovered that employees even wanted praise more than pay raises. Out of this research came the theory of "Management by Walking Around" (MBW) – a theory that Dave Packard and Bill Hewlett of Hewlett-Packard, Inc. strongly embraced and proved to be successful. The concept of one-minute with God each hour might also prove successful.

What does a 'One Minute Believer" do? Taking this concept to the marketplace is "being present" with the Lord, praising the Lord, and depending on Him throughout the day.

Your daily tasks or challenges become a part of your one-minute per hour communion with God. Your relationship with Him is as close as your breath.

"Lord, please be with me on this client call," "Lord, go before me to prepare the way, and give me the words and boldness to speak to my boss," "Lord, thank you for protecting me in that situation," or "Lord, that person has been on my mind, I lift her up in prayer and ask for protection, health, and wisdom in her life right now, in Jesus' name. Amen."

The "big lie" in our fast-paced marketplace world is that 1) we do not have time for effective prayer, and 2) effective prayer takes a long time. The result is, we do not pray.

One-minute prayers are powerful. In the book, *Overcoming Overload,* authors Steve and Mary Farrar list "Seven Ways to Find Rest in Your Chaotic World." The following are their comments on prayer:

Prayer is the escape vehicle that lets you decompress from the pressures of life. It provides oxygen for the soul. Without it, your spiritual life will become cold and dead. Without it, you will eventually succumb, and 'overload' will claim another victim. A prayerless person is like someone who eats and sleeps but forgets to breathe! He is a person who does not walk with God.

I watched a television show on brain waves. When we are calm and still, our brain waves from the back of the brain begin to align with the brain waves from the front of the brain, and a consistent pattern develops. Within a few minutes, all parts of the brain are communicating with each other.

Research shows that this kind of relaxation, meditation, peacefulness, and stillness, increases innovation, test scores, productivity, energy, and much more. It also opens our hearts and minds to direction from the Lord.

Take a deep breath, and breathe out a prayer of thanksgiving in the name of Jesus right now, and feel His strength, peace, and wisdom flow through. Take a minute or more for stillness and prayer in your life.

Keep It Simple

Do not deceive yourselves. If anyone of you thinks he is wise by the standards of this age, he should become a "fool" so that he may become wise. For the wisdom of this world is foolishness in God's sight. As it is written: He catches the wise in their craftiness.

1 Corinthians 3:18-19

Jesus said, "I thank You, Father . . .that You have hidden these things from the wise and clever…and revealed them to babies" (Matthew 11:25). I am so thankful for this Scripture, because I was a "baby" in religious and educational thought when I accepted Jesus as my Savior at age twenty-three. I had no Christian religious training and a limited education.

The Holy Spirit trained and taught me from the Word of God and through personal revelation in my spirit for three years before I found a church. God calls the wisdom of the philosophers and intellectuals "foolish" because they deny the power of God.

I once heard a professor say she would not receive a paper from a student debating evolution versus creation, because the only book the student could use was the Bible, and she does not consider the Bible a scholarly reference. How incredulous is that? When I was on a school board, the American Civil Liberties Union (ACLU) came to our board meeting and said, "They did not want children praying over their food at lunch time, because it took away the freedoms of the other children."

What about the freedom of the children who wanted to bless their food? In the political arena, God's wisdom is rarely invited in to the decision-making process. Where is the wisdom in spending millions to save whales, while at the same time fighting for the right to kill unborn human babies?

Jesus said, "Unless you change and become like little children, you will never enter the kingdom of heaven" (Matthew 18:3, NIV). We must have the heart of a child, not intellectual superiority, to receive the hidden messages of God. When you reach out to others– keep it simple.

Personal Growth in the Desert

Now it came to pass in those days, when Moses was grown, that he went out to his brethren and looked at their burdens. And he saw an Egyptian beating a Hebrew, one of his brethren. So he looked this way and that way, and when he saw no one, he killed the Egyptian and hid him in the sand.

Exodus 2:11

There are so many things that encourage me about the life of Moses. First, he was adopted and was not raised by his loving Hebrew family. But as painful as those circumstances seem, God had a special plan to train Moses in the way of the Egyptians.

Second, he murdered someone, an unthinkable sin to most of us, yet God used him in a most remarkable way as a great leader. Finally, it is confirmed to my heart once again that his long wilderness experience after the murder was not just an exile, but also an opportunity to spend time with God and be stripped of all self.

It was not an abandonment of Moses by God, but rather it was a calling from God to draw close to Him. Once again we are being reminded to not get ahead of God (like Moses) and do things within our own design or power.

In the Bible, Acts 2:46 records that day after day the Christians regularly assembled and took communion. Bruce Wilkinson, in *Secrets of the Vine,* discusses abiding in the Lord. "Abiding begins with visible spiritual discipline, such as Bible reading and prayer. Yet amazingly, we can do these things for years without abiding."

Wilkinson points out that reading the book is not the same as knowing the one who wrote it. He suggests that we speak less, listen for Him, mediate on His Word, write down what we hear Him saying to us, and make time for an honest, deep, and intimate communication time.

Time in the desert gives us opportunity to yield over to God wrong attitudes, unbelief, offenses, and fear. It is a time for communion with God to draw from His Grace. It is also a time to prepare for the next opportunity or calling that is about to come your way.

Enjoy the desert experience. It is a time for personal growth, character building, and strengthening.

Signing Away My Rights

I have been crucified with Christ; and it is no longer I who live, but Christ lives in me…

Galatians 2:20 NASB

I have never seen anyone sign away his or her rights to a greater degree than my husband. When I completed my first book, *School Boards – A Call to Action,* I had an opportunity to go to a conference in Denver and possibly have an informal meeting with the leadership of an organization called Christian Voice to see if they would consider the publication and distribution of my book.

While I was packing, my husband came to me and said, "The Lord wants me to tell you that whatever they ask you to do, say 'Yes.' Do not call me and ask for permission. I release you to negotiate whatever it takes to get this book out there." He adamantly made me promise that I would demonstrate my leadership and confidence and not call him.

At the conference, after a day and a night, the meeting was not taking place. I went to my room to pray. Suddenly I heard in my spirit, "Take the book and go down the escalator now!" I rushed out of the room to the main escalator. Coming up the other side was the president of the organization and his advisor. I said, "Would this be a good time to meet?"

He replied, "Yes, wait downstairs in the coffee shop, I'll be right there." I told him my school board story, gave him the book, and asked him to consider publishing it.

Another day passed, and the call came. "Could you meet the leadership of our organization in our conference suite immediately?" I sat before three men, listening to their proposal.

I remembered what my husband said just as the question came: "We need to know if you will commute to Washington, D.C. (from Washington State) and live there at our expense for 10 to 15 days per month for at least a year to promote the book and develop an education task force?"

After a short pause, I replied with great confidence, "Yes."

They asked, "Don't you need to call your husband?" They then listened in amazement as I told them what he said, and I explained we were BOTH called to this vision.

For several years, my husband held down the home front, as this education task force evolved into the American Parents Association, and the book was distributed in all 50 states.

I wrote this devotion on November 1 - our wedding anniversary to honor a man who signed away his rights for me and for God.

Letting Go and Letting God

In blessing I will bless you and in multiplying I will multiply your descendants like the stars of the heavens and the sand on the seashore. And your Seed (Heir) will possess the gate of His enemies.

Genesis 22:17

Many Christians (and Jews and Arabs) know this verse/promise to Abraham about his descendants being multiplied. Why did God make such a huge promise to him? In the previous verse, the Lord says, "Since you have done this and have not withheld (from Me) or begrudged (giving Me) your son, your only son" (Genesis 22:16).

Abraham received this promise because He OBEYED God's voice and was willing to sacrifice his son. Just before the knife went into Abraham's son's heart, an Angel of the Lord called to him from heaven and told him to stop (verse 11) and a voice said "I know that you fear and revere God, since you have not held back from me" (Genesis 22:12).

A friend of mine recently mentioned that God did not stop Abraham as soon as he determined in his heart to obey, or when he was walking up the mountain, or even when he tied up his son and took hold of the knife. God intervened when he was actually carrying out what he was called to do.

I remember 30 years ago reading this story and realizing I had to give my three children to God. At first I thought, "no problem my Lord, my children are Yours."

But then when I realized that meant ANYTHING could happen, even their death, it took me days to wrestle with the Lord my will versus His will. Finally that weekend, on the side of a hill at a park, watching my children play below, sobbing before God, I gave Him my children and said "I trust you with their lives."

A famous preacher once said that the reason we do not trust God is because we evaluate God by our character, and we do not understand His character. We can only interpret what God is doing through our own life experiences.

My children did not die, but as I watched them go through trying and challenging experiences with their own faith being tested, I was able to have complete confidence and trust in the One who created them.

What is really exciting about what Abraham did is that we are the ones that benefit from his obedience. Verse 18 says "And in your Seed (Christ) shall all the nations of the earth be blessed and (by Him) bless themselves, because you have heard and obeyed My voice."

Because of Abraham, we received Jesus Christ from his descendants, and we receive all the blessings of being grafted into that family tree as Christians. As we obey God, we can also believe that our heritage of blessings will pass on to our children and grandchildren.

Thank you, Abraham, for being willing to give your only son. Thank you, God, for giving your only Son. Thank you, Jesus, for giving your life for me. May I live worthily and in obedience to God to honor the sacrifices paid centuries before me.

It is Finished

By one offering He has perfected forever those who are being sanctified.
Hebrews 10:14 NKJV

"It is finished." Those were the words of Our Lord Jesus on the cross. In the Scripture above, it says that He FOREVER perfected us. There isn't anything left to do but to accept what Jesus did for us.

In addition to salvation through Jesus, I have heard the terms "sanctification" and "redemption." Sanctification is "the state of growing in divine grace as a result of Christian commitment or conversion." Redemption is "to repair or restore; to change for the better; to make good; to overcome; or to be set free from captivity with a ransom."

In other words, salvation through Jesus is a daily ongoing, growing experience. I can trust that Jesus is working in my life every day to make me more like Him. In Hebrews 10:14, the Scripture says, "by one offering" He made us perfect.

My perfection may be ongoing, but my resources to obtain everything I need are complete and available through Jesus. To be full of wisdom, to be confident, competent, loving, forgiving, or an effective leader, can only be done through Him.

Too many Christians are not allowing Jesus to complete His work in them. They believe, they are saved, but they are not yielded daily to the power (or correction) of God that changes us, makes us better, and makes us overcome.

Starting each day with a yielding prayer will invite God's redemptive power to work in us. I need the fruits of the Holy Spirit to succeed, and I can only receive fruit on my branches if I abide in the Vine (Jesus). When I spend time with Jesus first thing in the morning, I can draw on those gifts to face the day.

But do not wait until tomorrow morning if you are reading this – pray now!

> *Lord Jesus, I in my own strength cannot face the day ahead. I thank you, Jesus, that you are within me and you empower me to*

be successful. Through You I can be made ready for the tasks that are put before me. Through you I can be gentle and kind. I ask that Your strength and wisdom pour through me today and this week, and I receive your promise of inner strength according to Philippians 4:13 that says,: "I have strength for all things in Christ who empowers me. I am ready for anything through Him who infuses inner strength into me: I am self- sufficient in Christ's sufficiency." I ask these things in Your Name. Amen.

When Jesus said, "It is finished," He was telling us that everything He wanted to provide for us is now available. He has given us everything we need to succeed if we draw from Him.

Naturally Good

Those who are Christ's have crucified the flesh with its passions and desires.
Galatians 5:24 NKJV

I used to envy people who were naturally good. They did not get into trouble at school, they got along with their parents, they behaved properly and gracefully in public settings, morality was easy for them, they were active and respected in their churches, and happy in their marriage.

Yet I noticed that over the years, their natural goodness kept them from acknowledging they needed Jesus Christ as their Savior. For many of these people, the thought of the thief on the cross entering paradise is difficult to accept, and the possibility of a murderer on death row entering heaven is incomprehensible.

To deny yourself and come unto Jesus means to let go of your natural ability to do good. I hate the sins, failures, and pain of my past, but those very things brought me to the foot of the cross and enabled me to experience His forgiveness. The fact that I had nothing but brokenness to bring to Him, makes the power of His love so much greater.

Do you ever hit a wall of trying to do things right, and they just keep going wrong? Every time I hit that wall, I have to completely let go, and once again come to the realization that only by the grace of God do I walk accurately and excellently before Him. The following has been my marketplace prayer:

> *"Lord, I yield myself completely to you. I give this day to you, and I trust You with my life. Everything that is about to happen to me today, I accept by Your design, and I thank you for the grace and wisdom to handle every circumstance. I completely let go, and I give you my assignments, my time management, my interpersonal relationships, my workload, and my success.*

> *If anything good happens today, it will be because of You, and I give You all the glory. I have tried, but without You, trying is not enough. I have used my natural gifts and talents, but without You, natural gifts are not enough. I have strived to be excellent, but*

without You, I will fail. My motives are pure, and I want to do a good job for You.

Be with me today. I put on the armor of God, and I lift up my shield of faith and the sword of the Spirit as I go forth today with You by my side and with You as my protector. I can only play a few notes, but with you as my conductor, I can play a symphony. Amen."

A continued brokenness and dependency on Him is our greatest strength.

The Heart of the Matter

I did not come to bring peace, but a sword.

Matthew 10:34 NIV

This Scripture about the sword is often used to explain how Jesus divides families when people accept Him or how nations fight against nations because of the Christian faith. It can also mean how a sword of truth pierces our heart through testing and trials making us more Christ-like.

The sword of Jesus is like a surgical instrument, removing those things that keep us from walking in complete freedom. Every painful truth about myself that I have had to face has blossomed into a beautiful garden of growth in the Lord.

For example, many years ago, a sister-in-the-Lord told me that she was burdened by the fact that I talked about my poverty all the time. She said that if I did not break the pattern of negative confession and curses of poverty over my family, I would never be able to enter in to the blessings and prosperity the Lord had for me.

I certainly was not walking in faith, and I knew in my heart that she was speaking the truth. It took me a full year to get the victory over my mouth and to praise God for our blessings, even when there were very few. Jesus came with a sword, and the spirit of poverty was broken off of my family that year.

It took courage for my friend to get to the heart of the matter. I cried when my friend allowed the Lord to speak the truth through her, but looking back at my life, I now rejoice that Jesus came with a sword.

In Rick Joyner's book, *The Final Quest,* he describes these moments as coming before the Judgment Seat of Christ and asking God what things in our heart or mind do we need to lay at the altar. If we come willingly, then maybe Jesus will not have to come with a sword to remove them.

Get Alone with Jesus

As soon as He was alone, His followers, along with the twelve began asking Him about the parables.

Mark 4:10

Heartbreak, disappointment, sickness, and broken friendships drive us to be alone with Jesus. We think we have all the answers until our world falls apart. Our stubbornness causes us to want to do things our way instead of the Lord's way, and our ignorance keeps us from understanding the danger of that kind of a walk.

Getting alone with Jesus provides an opportunity for prayer and allows the Holy Spirit to work on our attitudes. If we allow the Holy Spirit to be honest with us, we will realize that perhaps we have been reacting with irritability to our spouses or family members, whining and complaining, or having negative feelings toward someone.

We blindly think we can move forward in life with these issues – no big deal. But our loving Father knows they will trip us up and cause us to fall, so He allows certain circumstances to bring us back to Him.

I heard a speaker at a Campus Crusade for Christ conference say, "I was an excellent 'poser' – I knew how to pose as a Christian." He explained that he knew how to do all the right things to look like a Christian, but in his heart and in many of his secret behaviors, he was far away from God.

He fooled everyone enough to even be asked to lead a college-age church group. Very difficult circumstances brought him on his face before God. He not only had to get honest with Jesus, he went to the church leadership and confessed that he was a fake.

Instead of rejecting him, they put him under church discipleship and trained him into the leader God wanted him to be. Today, he serves in a powerful way by the grace of God, and lives are changed through his full-time ministry.

God loved him too much to leave him in his vast state of stubbornness and ignorance. When you see other people in struggles, a good prayer is, "Lord, use this situation to get this person alone with You."

Your Best Friend

The thief comes only to steal and kill and destroy; I came that they may have life, and have it abundantly. I am the good shepherd; the good shepherd lays down his life for his sheep.

John 10:10-13 NASB

There is an old hymn that says, "What a friend we have in Jesus." Did you ever stop to think what that means to those of us in the marketplace/workplace? It means, along with the Father and the Holy Spirit, He's the only one we can trust.

Co-workers and managers for the most part are not looking out for your best interest in the workplace, but Jesus is. You can confide in Him, and He will comfort and sustain you. He will pray with you. He will guide you in your work relations, He will listen to you, and He will protect you. He loves you!

I sense in my spirit that many who are reading this are wondering if God is going to expand your borders or enlarge your influence. Yes, He is! He is in the expansion business.

Status quo and comfort zones are never part of his plan. If you are praying for God to expand your territory or believing for a promotion, I encourage you to read *The Prayer of Jabez* by Bruce Wilkinson. Jabez in the Bible had the exact same prayer, and it was answered!

Perhaps some of you are having your responsibilities and influence expanded faster than you think you are ready for, or you are afraid to take on more. Bruce Wilkinson assures us that our Lord, our best friend, will work in surprising ways:

He will arrange circumstances and opportunities that are more strategic for you;

He will become your scheduler;

You won't get more hours in your day, but you will find more effective ways of using the hours you are given;

The Spirit will show you ways to double your effectiveness and leverage opportunities in the most ordinary moments; and

You will notice that as some of your borders expand, others will shrink.

He already gave His life for you, and He wants to give you so much more. In John 10, Jesus continues to say that the good shepherd would leave the sheep to chase after the wolf, but the hireling will flee, "because he is a hireling, and cares not for the sheep" (v. 13) Remember, Jesus will not flee from you.

Consider the Trees

Blessed is the man who walks not in the counsel of the ungodly, nor stands in the path of sinners, nor sits in the seat of the scornful; but his delight is in the law of the Lord, and in His law he meditates day and night. He shall be like a tree planted by the rivers of water, that brings forth its fruit in its season, whose leaf also shall not wither; and whatever he does shall prosper.

Psalm 1: 1-4 NKJV

Consider the trees by the river – they are well provided for, fruitful, and full of life. Whether you are poor or rich, worrying about the cares of the world will wither you up and make you useless for God's work.

My husband and I spent most of our lives with a poverty mentality, completely preoccupied with how we were going to make ends meet. I swear, the more we worried about it, the poorer we became.

When we changed our focus on serving, giving, and trusting Him, we realized one day that all our needs were being met. In *Secrets of the Vine*, Bruce Wilkinson writes, "The secret of true abundance is to want what God wants."

There is so much debate about today's evangelical prosperity messages. If you are listening to the ones about God's will for you to drive a Lexus and live in a palace, then you are listening to ones that are focusing on things and not on God. God's prosperity is health, provision, spiritual growth, and expansion of ministry.

In 1 Chronicles 4:9-10, a man by the name of Jabez prayed. He asked to move him out of "pain" (the meaning of his name) and to move him into honor. He asked for God to expand his territories and to bless him. And God answered his prayer!

If you are not thinking about how you can expand your territory for God and fulfill your mission on this earth, then your prayer for wealth may be amiss. If you are not meditating on the things of God as listed in the Psalm above, then your prayers may not be answered.

I am reminded of a story that Wilkinson shares in his book, *Beyond Jabez,* where a daughter of Christian parents was a drug addict and always angry at God. When she finally was sober for a year and gave her life completely to God, she prayed the prayer of Jabez and asked God to bless her, expand her territory, get her out of debt, and help her start her life over.

Two weeks later a check arrived for $76,000 from an injury lawsuit that had been filed years earlier. She praised God for His timing because if she had received the blessing sooner, she would have spent it all on drugs.

God does want to prosper us in many ways – and He has the right timing for our lives. Your job is to be a tree planted by the river of life – Jesus.

Give God a Chance

"If you will return, O Israel'" says the Lord...

Jeremiah 4:1 NKJV

I cannot judge the decisions others make at the crossroads of life whether they choose obedience to God or self-will, nor can I boast and say that I have chosen better. This I can say – every crossroad is a battle of the mind and the will, and unless we win our private battle alone with God and settle matters once and for all, we will always lose our external battles that are visible to others.

I believe every married couple today will face the crossroads of divorce. Every force in hell has come against marriage and family. The destruction of the family has destroyed the very fabric of our society.

The prisons are filled with drug addicts and murderers who will tell you they had no family life. Statistics say that three out of every four marriages will fail.

When I see couples go through the challenge of separation and divorce, I want to cry out, "Give God a chance!" But I know from multiple past experiences, their hearts are already hardened. Their wills are already set in stone. The battle was lost way before it ever got to this point. The only road back is a complete brokenness and a letting go of self and desiring God's will, not their own desires.

My marriage has been at a crossroads several times over the past thirty-seven years. We were not Christians when we married; we were extremely immature, complete opposites, and we got married out of loneliness in the military, not out of love.

After we became Christians, we decided it was God's will to make it work. All our friends who witnessed the first twenty-five years can testify that it is a miracle that we are together. At one point in our marriage there was a serious separation, but we came back together because "it was what God wanted us to do" – not because we had wonderful feelings of love and reconciliation. All our hopes and emotions for a better future came later.

The good news is, once we had overcome the battle of the will, all of Satan's attacks were powerless after that. When people ask how we stayed together for so long, we reply with one word – "Forgiveness." Now looking back, I believe there is another word – "brokenness" – brokenness of our self-will.

The Bible says that God does not "till the ground forever" and now there is a harvest of love and joy in our marriage. God's arm is not too short for even the worst situation. In fact – He loves the impossible. Give God a chance.

Pour from the Overflow

...separated to the gospel of God...

Romans 1:1 NKJV

The Spirit of the Lord has impressed on my heart to tell others to not pour themselves out to others (in ministry or in our jobs) to such a degree that the well of our soul becomes dry. Rather pour from "our overflow" – from the abundance of spending time with God.

Apostle Paul was one of the greatest Christians who ever walked the earth. He endured suffering, he traveled extensively, he was content, he had joy, he was the Apostle of the original churches, he wrote numerous epistles, he preached, and he spread the Gospel wherever he went. Yet, he rarely spoke of his character or his accomplishments and he never mentioned weariness.

He always spoke of Jesus, and he regularly mentioned how he separated himself to God. His eyes were not focused on his own personal holiness or tasks – but rather on the mission God had given him and on his relationship with God.

Many Christian churches have failed to be powerful and effective, because people focus on their own holiness and the holiness of others, rather focusing on their desire to know God. If we were all focused on God, and not on others, there would be an overflow of love, salvation, and healing that would spread throughout the land.

In the marketplace, in our churches, and in our homes, we are being stretched in multiple directions. With increased responsibilities, world stresses, high self-expectations, new technologies, it sometimes seems more than we can endure. Women, in particular, are balancing home, church, and career in ways that previous generations have not endured.

I am not saying if you should take on more or if there is something you need to let go of. Those decisions are between you and the Lord.

What I am saying is if you spend more time with your Creator and His Son, there will be an overflow so that you will be able to pour out without draining your spirit and your strength. Remember that Jesus offered the woman at the well living water, water that would keep her from ever being thirsty (John 4:5-15).

If you spend time with God, HE will let you know what to let go of and what to take on. If He gives you an assignment, He promised that, "His yoke is easy, and His burden is light" (Matthew 11:30, NKJV).

I realize now, that when Jesus turned the water into wine, the greater miracle was "it never ran out!" Meditate on these truths from God:

"Let all who take refuge in (God) be glad" (Psalm 5:11, NKJV).

"Your faith should not stand in the wisdom of men, but on the power of God" (1 Corinthians 2:5, KJV)

"Not by might, not by power, but by my Spirit, says the Lord" (Zechariah 4:6, NKJV)

May God bless the work of your hands and give you strength, wisdom, and peace today.

A Burning Heart for Jesus

Then opened He their understanding, that they might understand the Scriptures.

Luke 24:45 KJV

The very day of the resurrection, two disciples (followers of Jesus, not the Apostles) were walking toward Emmaus, a town located about seven miles from Jerusalem, conversing about the weekend events. Talk about the ultimate debriefing!

Suddenly Jesus Himself caught up with them, but the Lord did not allow them to recognize Him. When Jesus heard their tale of discouragement, that the One they believed would deliver Israel from the Romans was dead, and His body was missing, He said to them, "O foolish ones (sluggish in mind, dull of perception) and slow of heart to believe (adhere to and trust in and rely on) everything that the prophets have spoken! Was it not necessary and essentially fitting that the Christ, (the Messiah) should suffer all these things before entering into His glory (His majesty and splendor)?" (Luke 24: 25-26).

Then as He walked with them, "beginning with Moses and (throughout) all the Prophets, He went on explaining and interpreting to them in all the Scriptures the things concerning and referring to Himself" (v. 27).

When they reclined at a table to break bread together, and He blessed it, "their eyes were instantly opened and they clearly recognized Him, and He vanished" (v. 31).

It was at this point that they said, "Were not our hearts greatly moved and burning within us while He was talking with us on the road and as He opened and explained to us (the sense of) the Scriptures?" (v. 32).

As with the disciples, our day-to-day commonplace duties can smother the burning heart we first had when we met Jesus, Our Savior. Often, we make promises to God, and then lose enthusiasm in the everyday stresses of life.

We forget Jesus' comforting words, "Abide in Me, and I (will abide) in you" (John 15:4, NASB) The two disciples ran back to Jerusalem to report their experience to the Apostles, and the Apostles confirmed to them that Jesus had really risen and appeared to Peter.

As they were talking, Jesus stood among them and said, "Peace be to you" (Luke 24:36, NASB), and then He asked for something to eat. The Apostles and disciples were startled with fear and thought Jesus was a ghost.

He once again went through the Scriptures with them, concerning everything that had been written about Him. "Then He opened their minds to understand the Scriptures" (v. 45, NASB). After this encounter, they understood that they would be witnesses of His death and resurrection, preaching forgiveness of sins, to all nations.

Do you need a renewed burning heart? Go into the Scriptures with Jesus.

Allow the Holy Spirit to quench your thirsty spirit and give you fresh living waters in the valley of life. Experience the joy of a daily encounter with Him.

Part 6
Strength, Balance and Wisdom

Entering His Rest

…and I will give you rest.

Matthew 11: 28 NASB

Self-awareness of our internal feelings makes us anxious, but God putting His awareness in us gives us peace. One thing that God wants us to do is to fight the good fight of faith in order to enter His rest.

Did you ever wonder how Jesus slept through a storm that was flooding and sinking the boat? His disciples, in complete fear, had to wake Him up!

He had perfect rest because He knew God's presence, and He knew that His God would take care of Him (Mark 4:35-40). Hebrews 6:19-20 talks about how Jesus is the anchor of our souls when we go through a storm, and it talks about entering into the certainty of His Presence within the veil.

Sounds like an umbrella of hope and peace to me – but we have to choose to get under His presence. In Hebrews Chapters 3 and 4, there is also an explanation of entering into God's rest.

The first rest described by Paul was the Israelites NOT entering into the promised rest, because they were rebellious with their grumbling, complaining, and lack of faith in God's promises.

The second rest is the promised rest we will receive when we enter heaven into the final Sabbath-rest, and we cease from the weariness and pain of human labors (Hebrews 4:8-10).

The third and last rest is to enter into God's rest here on earth. The Hebrew translation for entering God's rest is "cease and abide."

We need to cease unbelief, grumbling, and complaining in our storms of life, and we need to abide – draw close to the throne of God's unmerited favor and grace – to receive peace.

How do we do that? Through seeking Jesus in prayer, spending time in praise and worship, and reading the Word of God to find His promises. Are you worried about something? Then meditate on Philippians 4:6-7:

"Do not fret or have any anxiety about anything, but in every circumstance and in everything, by prayer and petition (definite requests), with thanksgiving, continue to make your wants know to God. And God's peace shall be yours - that tranquil state of a soul assured of its salvation through Christ, and so fearing nothing from God and being content with its earthly lot of whatever sort that is, that peace which transcends all understanding shall garrison and mount guard over your hearts and minds in Christ Jesus" (Amplified).

If we try to overcome our circumstances with increased self-awareness through any of our own commonsense methods, we will only strengthen our self-awareness and increase our fears and anxiety. Jesus invites, "Come to Me, all you who are weary and burdened, and I will give you rest" (Matthew 11:28, NIV)

In the second storm the disciples went through Jesus said, as He stood on a violent sea of waves, "Take heart! I AM! Stop being alarmed and afraid!" (Mark 6:50).

Entering God's rest is not being in denial. It is not a method of avoiding the pain. It does not mean that you do not make critical and rational decisions. It is God's method of helping us survive or to walk on the water of the rough seas.

I love the fact that when Peter walked on the water toward Jesus, he had faith. When his faith wavered, he began to sink, but Jesus grabbed him and lifted him up, and they walked back to the boat together. We always think that Peter failed, when in fact, when he got his eyes back on Jesus, he finished the task successfully.

The Second Mile

But I say to you, do not resist an evil person; but whoever slaps you on your right cheek, turn the other to him also.

Matthew 5:39 NASB

In the *Sermon on the Mount,* Jesus teaches that if a soldier asks you to carry his equipment for a mile, offer to carry it *a second mile.* So often we think about our rights – our rights to refuse to take that kind of treatment, our rights to refuse to work with that person, our rights to refuse to submit to that boss, or our rights to refuse to work on an assignment that is not in our job description. Our only right is to represent the Lord Jesus Christ.

I am the first to admit this is all easier said than done and with each challenge there is a process we go through. I think most people are just so stressed at work, they just do not know how to interact in positive ways anymore. The corporate world has sucked the life and souls out of their human resources, and it has reduced the workforce to a life of drudgery and non-creativity.

One trainer, Michael Jones, brings music and a piano into his management workshops. Jones maintains, "The corporation's new story needs to come from the inside out. Companies have to redefine the organizational contract so that we can bring artistry into our work again."

David Whyte, a poet, engages corporate employees in poetic conversations and uses poets like Robert Frost to soften the hardcore leaders of companies like Boeing, AT&T, and Shell Oil. He made a powerful statement that I believe we can apply to our role in the workplace while we are turning the other cheek: "On their side is cynicism and on my side are all the great names of world literature. I have to work to establish a connection, but eventually one is made. I don't try to overcome resistance; I put the weight on the conversation, and let it do all the work." There lies the key in these tough relationships that want to rob our peace and joy.

How can we overcome resistance? By allowing God to use our conversation and let it do all the work. By spending time with Him and in His word so that in that very hour the Holy Spirit will give us the words and we can ever so gently, laying down all our rights, build conversations that may unfold into the peace and joy they are looking for.

I believe in these days of high pressure in the workplace we are going to: 1) have more demands put on us, and it is going to be tempting to react; 2) need to keep our vessel full of God himself in order to turn the other cheek and go the extra mile; 3) be asked of God to show a peace that others do not have, so that they will be drawn to us; and 4) find creative ways to bring God's artistry, creativity, beauty, and refreshment to the workplace.

Some great ideas for the summer months are: bring fresh flowers to work, give a plant to your support staff or boss, hang a painting on the wall that brings inspiration, take cool drinks to work, or order lunch for the office.

One summer, an employee went out in the 117-degree desert heat and brought everyone in the office a treat from Dairy Queen. He went the extra mile.

I wish I had thought of that one! Ask God to give you something memorable and refreshing to do for your co-workers or neighbors.

It's Just a House

"I have finished the work which You have given Me to do."
John 17:4 NKJV

There are three kinds of surrender – surrender of our possessions, surrender of circumstances, and surrender of our will. All of us must come to a place where we can say, "If I lost my car, my job, my house, or everything, I will still be grateful to have my life, and I will still love God."

The victims of hurricane Katrina reached to their hardships in a way that demonstrated they understood what really matters in life. Max Lucado writes, "As you've listened to evacuees and survivors, have you noticed their words? No one laments a lost plasma television or submerged SUV. No one runs through the streets yelling, 'My cordless drill is missing' or 'My golf clubs have washed away.' If they mourn, it is for people lost. If they rejoice, it is for people found."

When I start to worry too much about the landscape of the yard, the worn carpet, the chipped tile, or the noisy water heater, I can hear God saying, "It's just a house." I then refocus on Him and put those things in His hands and remember what really matters.

In the surrender of circumstances, we are really letting go and letting God give us rest. We give up trying to do it our way, and we ride with the uncertainty of our future, knowing that God has everything under control.

Working in the marketplace can be a daily surrender. John Maxwell in his book *Life @ Work* writes, "Our work somehow makes the world a better place. At the end of the day, if it is all about me and my money, then we have left something out: primarily, a service to humanity."

Surrender means to give our best efforts at work in an attitude of serving, even when we do not feel like it or when circumstances are tough. Surrender does not make things less in our lives – it makes things greater. "Work can either be something that shrinks me down to an even more self-centered existence, or it can open me up to the larger world around me" (Maxwell).

The third surrender is the surrender of our will. When God calls us to do something where people oppose and reject us and we have to walk the road all alone, that is a surrender of our will unto death - a death of "what will people think." Then people cannot hurt you anymore, because that area of your life is dead, and you know there is nothing that 'man' can do unto you ever again because you cannot kill a dead person twice! This is total surrender.

Yield whatever you are holding on to willingly in prayer now, so that when you do have to let go, it is not so heart wrenching. In a situation like "Katrina," I want to be that woman I saw on the news, walking in water up to her chest with a small bag of possessions, telling the press, "We're going to be fine. I praise God we have our lives and that is all that matters. God is good."

Taking Work Projects Captive

… bringing every thought into captivity to the obedience of Christ…
2 Corinthians 10:5 NKJV

According to a Moffatt translation of this verse, taking every thought into captivity means taking every project into captivity. Jesus was not impulsive. He took every thought and plan to His Father in prayer.

We sometimes even do Christian works impulsively, and it may be something that God did not ask us to do. Sometimes people start off in the right direction, obeying God's will, and then get easily distracted, sidetracked, or lose focus.

The best way to stay on track is to have a plan. Jesus had a plan, and He always gave instructions to his staff based on his plan. Laurie Beth Jones, author of *Jesus CEO,* writes: "He spoke often about how something was either part of or not part of the plan. He did not claim to know all the details, but He certainly saw the big picture and acted on a day-to-day basis according to inner instructions."

Jones asks the following questions: "What is your plan?" "Is it written down?" "Is it clear?" "Can it be communicated?" "Is it workable?" "How can you implement it?" and "When will you begin?"

After you have a clear plan, you must take time and priorities into captivity to the obedience of Christ. Stephen Covey first taught the concept of first things first. By doing second things first, we are not disciplining "our projects."

John Maxwell, author of *Leadership 101,* asks, "How come we can get 100 things done the week before a vacation and get our desk completely clean? Why can't we work like that every week?"

Probably because we work on things we like instead of things we need to do. "All true leaders learn to say no to the good in order to say yes to the best" (Maxwell).

Self-discipline takes practice and the yielding of those "I'll do it tomorrow" thoughts to the Lord when it can be done today. Always have a plan or long-term vision, but pray the following prayer daily, "Lord, help me to do today what *You* want me to work on to reach the goals You have given me."

Each day in the parking lot of my workplace before I start the tasks of the day, I pray, "Lord, help me to complete those things you would have me do, help me prioritize and not be distracted, and help me be sensitive to Your will. Help me to be excellent in all that I do for Your glory. Amen."

Seek the Source of the River

"He who believes in Me…out of his heart will flow rivers of living water."
John 7:38 NKJV

Typically, we teach leaders to pursue their goals, but Jesus said, "Pursue me." When a river comes to an obstacle, it will either make a pathway around it or drop out of sight sometimes going below the surface for miles.

If you feel that an obstacle has stopped your destiny, success, or calling, then go back to the source rather than focus on the obstacle. God will help you get around the obstacle or remove it, or He will let you know that it is time to go underground for some training or character building. You will also discover that it was the journey of obstacles and the humility of being unseen that created the rushing powerful "broader and greater" river.

Regarding your goals and God's purpose for your life, John Maxwell writes in *Life @ Work* that even though we do not necessarily know all the details, here is what we do know:

God operates off of a master plan, even though He does not always tell us what it is.

God specifically fits each of us as Christians into the larger workings of His overall plan.

We serve His purpose through faith by following our best understanding of His calling in our lives.

John Maxwell also points us to the source when he writes, "The problem is that many today live at work as a way of life. The job drives them, not the calling. Unless we understand that distinction, the job that Jesus calls us to can actually end up calling us away from Him" (Maxwell).

When a river meets an obstacle, it does not passively wait, it cautiously pursues the next course of action while it waits for additional water from its source, so that it can push through, around, or under to its final destination. Just keep your eye on the source and wait upon Him; before long, you will be flowing freely again.

Jesus Here and Now

Jesus said to him, "Because you have seen Me, Thomas, do you now believe? Blessed and happy and to be envied are those who have never seen Me, and yet have believed and adhered to and trusted in and relied on Me."
John 20:29

Our focus on the next experience with Jesus could be blocking the way to be of service to the Lord today. Instead of looking for God to exhibit Himself to us, we need to be open in our relationship with Him so that God can exhibit Himself in us and through us to others.

By understanding that the Lord is here now and very present in our hearts, we will stop looking for a manifestation of His presence. Jesus wants us to understand that He is as close as our breath and a very PRESENT help in trouble. He will not leave us or forsake us. He is not some future experience that we are waiting for.

I have to admit I have been guilty of thinking "God must not be working in this prayer right now because I don't feel anything." There have been many times when I have prayed for someone, taught a Bible study, given a speech, or written a devotional, and I have "experienced God." I believed that the feeling was confirmation of His presence, but the truth is God is always present, and nine times out of ten we are going to have to pray for someone in faith, standing on God's Word, without any spiritual confirmation or feeling.

Be steadfast in your job assignment, steadfast in your ministry, and steadfast in your relationship with God and others, even if you do not feel like it. Do not grow weary in doing well, and in due season He will reward you.

Remember, Jesus is within you at all times, and His anointing is always present and upon you whether you feel it or not. Stop looking for that "next experience" with Jesus, but rather look for that next person or situation and be available for His assignment.

Be A Mary, Not a Martha

Let be and be still, and know (recognize and understand) that I am God.
Psalm 46: 10

In 2005, while fasting and praying for a message that I was going to give to the ladies at my church, the Lord spoke to my heart and said, "Tell the women to slow down and be Mary, not a Martha." Here is the story from Luke 10:38-42:

> *As Jesus and his disciples were on their way, he came to a village where a woman named Martha opened her home to him. She had a sister called Mary, who sat at the Lord's feet listening to what he said. But Martha was distracted by all the preparations that had to be made. She came to him and asked, "Lord, don't you care that my sister has left me to do the work by myself? Tell her to help me!" Martha, Martha," the Lord answered, "you are worried and upset about many things, but only one thing is needed. Mary has chosen what is better, and it will not be taken away from her" (NIV).*

The Spirit-Filled Life Bible asks the reader to reflect on the following regarding this passage of Scripture:

- Do I take time to meet my Good Shepherd each day, letting Him tell me of His love, and cheering His heart with my interest in Him?

- What is my greatest concern, the thing about which most of all I want Christ's help?

- Do I heed Christ when He bids me to come away from the lions' den of temptation and dwell with Him?

- Am I willing to have the north wind of adversity blow upon me, if it will better fit me for Christ's presence and companionship?

- In my weariness from earthly cares, do I hesitate to answer when the Divine Shepherd knocks at my door, and so turn Him from me?

Visualize Jesus down the hallway and in a room of your heart sitting there all alone. He is waiting for you to come to Him, but you never come.

He paid this great price so that He could have fellowship with you, and you are too busy. He can see that you are going to end up in a crisis, because you are going too fast, and He wants to help carry your burden, but you don't give it to Him.

See yourself going into the chamber, wrapping your arms around Him, and feeling His comforting arms around you. Then have a conversation with Him, and let Him give you clear direction for your life. Let be, and be still.

God's Standard

For we walk by faith, not by sight.

2 Corinthians 5:7 NKJV

Moments of inspiration are gifts and surprises from God - but not the standard. With prayer and times of quietness, we can go about our daily business, walking in faith, knowing that God is with us, and being ready and aware for the moments we can bless people or hear God's wisdom.

If we are murmuring and complaining, we will not hear Him and others will not see Him. If we come on too strong with supernatural enthusiasm, others will only see us, not God. If we are looking for a supernatural sign, rather than spending time in His presence, we will miss our daily assignments and fail to do His will.

What is our daily assignment? "Be still, and know that I AM God" (Psalm 46:10, NIV). There is no set formula to handle the daily pressures of life, except to know God and wait on God.

"But those who wait for the Lord (who expect, look for, and hope in Him) shall change and renew their strength and power; they shall lift their wings and mount up (close to God) as eagles (mount up to the sun); they shall run and not be weary, they shall walk and not faint or become tired" (Isaiah 40: 31).

I believe this was the secret of Joseph who went from slave, to prisoner, to chief administrator, second only to Pharaoh. He was a slave and prisoner for thirteen years, and he completed his tasks with excellence and by faith, not looking at the circumstances.

Be still before God, wait upon His direction and final outcome, and He will equip you with everything you need today. Whatever you are going through let God complete His perfect work and build His standard in you.

A Fresh Vision

Where there is no vision (no redemptive revelation of God), the people perish; but he who keeps the law (of God, which includes that of man)—blessed (happy, fortunate, and enviable) is he.

Proverbs 29: 18

Moral inspiration gives us moral incentive to live a life of honesty and integrity. Without inspiration, people fall away from God.

Jesus inspired over 10,000 people when He delivered the *Sermon on the Mount.* Nehemiah inspired God's people with a sermon to build a wall, a follow-up sermon to stand and fight for their families and their city, and a final sermon to live by the law of the Lord. Mordecai moved Esther in a God- inspired speech to fulfill her calling and destiny and risk her life for God's people.

How could Daniel pray openly when there was a decree that if you did, it meant certain death? It was because he had vision – inspiration from God.

Our morals and principles will not be enough when called to obedience. Without revelation, we lose sight of God, and we begin to be reckless, participate in activities we know are wrong, pray less, and cease to invite God's vision in the little things of life. We begin to do things on our own ability without expecting God to give us a fresh look. Without vision, we perish.

Whenever I find myself complaining about circumstances, I know I am doing things in my own capabilities, and I have failed to invite God to give me a fresh vision. Whining and complaining leads to exhaustion, and this leads to physical health problems.

God says in Proverbs that life without His presence and insight leads to sin and death. When the burden gets too heavy and when I lose the joy of the Lord, I get back in His presence to catch His vision.

There are many ways people get back into the presence of God – fasting and prayer, listening to spiritual/educational teachings, attending an inspiring church service, taking communion, or seeking counsel from a pastor or friend. The fastest way I know to get back into the presence of

God is down on your knees and not getting up until you have a renewed vision.

The freshness and vitality you need for a new spiritual outlook can be found in the throne room of God. Come into that throne room by thanking Jesus for giving you that immediate access to the heavenly Father. Be blessed today with the vision of Nehemiah, the courage of Daniel, the faith of Esther, and the Words of Jesus.

Making the Most of Time

Be very careful, then, how you live—not as unwise, but as wise, making the most every opportunity, because the days are evil.

Ephesians 5:15-16 NIV

God believes in planning, and He wants us to get in the habit of a well-disciplined, time-managed lifestyle. Jesus tells us to think ahead: "Suppose one of you wants to build a tower. Will he not first sit down and estimate the cost to see if he has enough money to complete it?" (Luke14:28-32, NIV).

God wants to give us direction: "I (the Lord) will instruct you and teach you in the way you should go; I will counsel you with My eye upon you. " (Psalm 32:8). Finally, Apostle Paul writes: "Let all things be done decently and in order." (1 Corinthians 14: 40, NKJV)

There are three time management skills I teach my students: "Just Do It", "Break It Down" (into small size tasks), and "Have a To Do List." The root of these concepts can be found in the Bible and are part of the teachings of Franklin, creator of time management systems and materials.

Steven Covey, author of *Seven Habits of Highly Effective People,* has a more centered approach. He writes that if we have a compass in our life – clear vision and goals that guide us – and if we put "first things first" the tasks of life will come into alignment and order. Franklin and Covey are now merged as one company, as if to say both are important.

Doing our time management part is important for a normal day, but this generation needs something supernatural to face the busy stress-filled days of our 21st century lifestyle.

In fact, the latest description of 21st century managers is, "Superleaders." The only way we can be superleaders is to depend on a supernatural God.

Putting first things first in the Scripture means seeking first the kingdom of God – seeking Him and seeking His principles. It means being present with God, giving Him your burdens (and your to do list), and leaning your entire personality upon Him.

Multiple times in the past, I did not know how I was going to meet my timelines and deadlines, but through focusing on one day at a time and leaning on God for strength and guidance, everything came together, every single time. I cannot explain how it works, I only know what His Scripture says: "Now to Him who is able to do exceedingly abundantly above all that we ask or think, according to the power that works in us" (Ephesians 3: 20, NKJV).

God's Provision

I know how to be abased, and I know how to abound. Everywhere and in all things I have learned both to be full and to be hungry, both to abound and to suffer need. I can do all things through Christ who strengthens me.
Philippians 4:12-13 NKJV

For some reason, God's people have made the subject of prosperity controversial. Perhaps it is because of the misuse of money by some evangelists. Perhaps it is because people fear that money will turn Christians away from God.

I have decided for my life three things on this topic: 1) I will follow what God's Word says, not what man says; 2) I will use money to bless others and to expand the kingdom of God; and 3) I will not allow fear of poverty or fear of wealth to be a part of my life because fear is not of God.

Deuteronomy 8:18 says: "But you shall (earnestly) remember the Lord your God, for it is He Who gives you power to get wealth, that He may establish His covenant which He swore to your fathers, as it is this day."

Power is defined as ability, strength, influence, talent and authority. The job you have right now and your future promotions are important to God. He wants to bless the work of your hands so that you can bless others.

Many people have criticized Pastor/Evangelist Kenneth Copeland, because he teaches on prosperity. I believe he has preached some of the most powerful messages on this topic and caused us to recognize that Satan wants to keep us in poverty so that we cannot establish God's covenant on the earth.

In the following message, Copeland never spoke of prosperity as a materialistic goal:

> *Jesus never built a worldly empire for Himself. But that doesn't mean He was poor. It means He was the greatest giver Who ever walked the face of this earth—and it's about time we started following in His footsteps. Don't you ever let anyone tell you it's wrong to want to prosper. It's wrong for you not to want to prosper*

when that prosperity can mean the difference between heaven and hell for millions of people. Forget about your own little needs. Raise your vision and set your mind on giving to meet someone else's, on establishing God's covenant in the earth. Then stand fast in faith and get ready to enjoy the greatest prosperity you've ever known.

It is not money that it evil, it is the LOVE of money that is evil. Wealth is only wrong when you put material things before God.

Jesus never said a wealthy man could not enter the kingdom of heaven, He only said it would be hard for a wealthy man to give up his possessions for the kingdom of God.

God's Word confirms the importance of prosperity: "You will be made rich in every way so that you can be generous on every occasion, and through us your generosity will result in thanksgiving to God" (2 Corinthians 9:11, NIV).

"God is able to make all grace abound to you…so that you may have an abundance for every good deed…" (2 Corinthians 9:8, NASB), and "My God shall supply all your need according to his riches in glory by Christ Jesus" (Philippians 4:19, NKJV). Open your hearts and minds to what God wants to do through you.

Showroom Christians

Not that I have now attained (this ideal), or have already been made perfect, but I press onto lay hold of (grasp) and make my own, that for which Christ Jesus (the Messiah) has laid hold of me and made me His own
Philippians 3:12

After many years of trying to be a "good Christian," I finally figured out that "Wendy" could not do it, and I had to let Jesus be a Christian through me. God does not want perfect Christians to put in a showroom display for all to see. Instead, the only perfection we should be working on is our perfection with our relationship with Jesus.

There was one point in my life that I was broken and ashamed of my failure as a Christian. I was completely empty inside and felt like I would never have anything to give God again. In fact, I could not even imagine why He would even want to use me.

An evangelist looked at me one day in a prayer meeting and said, "Your vessel is completely drained out and empty, isn't it?"

I said with tears in my eyes, "Yes."

"Good!" he exclaimed! "Now God can finally pour Himself in you and use you!"

If we dwell in Him, His characteristics will begin to pour out of us, and others will be drawn to HIM because of this relationship - not because of our so-called perfect Christianity. In fact, it is Christians judging others in the Christian showroom that is driving people away from God today.

People are hungry for something real, relevant, and loving in their lives and only Jesus can give that. Spend time with God in the morning, and then let Him be real, relevant, and loving to others through you throughout the day. My prayer is to not be "full of myself" but to be full of God.

I Call You Friend

Jesus replied, "Have I been with all of you for so long a time, and do you not recognize and know me yet, Philip?"

John 14:9

In our lifetime, we all look for that "best friend we can trust" and rarely find it. Moses spoke to God as a friend (Exodus 33:11), and Jesus spoke to His disciples as friends (John 15:15).

Jesus instructs us to make our friendship with God become our first priority. When He said, "Seek ye first the kingdom of God and all these things will be added unto you" – He did not just mean to seek the principles of God's kingdom – He wanted us to seek God in an intimate relationship.

In fact, He laid His life down for his friends so that we could be reunited with God. That was His ultimate goal.

There are wonderful benefits from developing a personal relationship with Jesus and the Father. God told Moses following their face-to-face meeting, "My presence shall go with you, and I will give you rest" (Exodus 33:14).

The sign of a close friendship with God is our peace. Everything will pass away, but our friendship with Jesus will last for all eternity.

God is so great, powerful, and awesome, it is difficult to picture Him as our friend. But He was a friend to Adam and Eve as He walked and talked with them in the Garden. Abraham was called the "friend of God" (James 2:23). God became man on earth to show us His love and friendship and to restore that relationship.

There is great evidence in the Bible of God's desire to be our friend. I want to be God's friend in return, and I have studied in the Word the characteristics of a friend.

How can we be God's friend? James 4:4 tells us that, "Whoever wishes to be a friend of the world makes himself an enemy of God" (NASB) Proverbs 17:17 explains that a friend loves at all times.

Jesus also instructed us that the measure of a true friend is his willingness to lay down his life for others. "Greater love has no one than this, than to lay down ones life for his friends. You are my friends, if you do whatever I command you" (John 15:13-14, NKJV).

To be a friend with Jesus is to be a friend to others. Jesus also said that He is our friend, because He shared everything with us and made the Father known to us (John 15:15). That means, as His friend, He wants us to share everything with Him.

The Trust Sacrifice

Abraham built an altar…and bound Isaac his son and laid him on the altar…
Genesis 22: 9

Many Christians have been challenged by the thought, "if I had to choose between renouncing the name of Jesus and living, would I be willing to die for Him?"

The early Christians had to make that choice in the face of Roman law and punishment. Christians in the Soviet Union were at one time imprisoned for holding underground church services. As commendable as being willing to die or being imprisoned for Christ is, living fully for Christ is what God requires of most of us.

In the story of Abraham regarding the sacrifice of his son, God did not want His son, He only wanted Abraham's will. Also, it was clear that God did not just want his sacrificial "works," because God provided a sacrificial animal to replace Abraham's son. This example was an advance revelation of what Jesus Christ was going to do for us.

Whatever we give God in our lives or through our lives, it is going to be through the death, blood, and grace of Jesus Christ. Our sacrifice is being willing to do it God's way.

In the marketplace, there is nothing more frustrating than not being able to implement creative ideas or run an organization the way you think it should be run. In fact, if we let it affect us, it becomes a weight that creates feelings of being in a rut or "stuck forever."

God is bigger than any weight, and He is our source of creativity, promotion, and leadership. Psalm 75:6 -7 says, "For not from the east nor from the west nor from the south come promotion and lifting up, but God is the judge! He puts down one and lifts up another."

When we recognize that He is a sovereign God in our life, and we let Him take the throne of our life, then He can work with us, through us, and for us even in the most limiting situations. It is our trust in God in the midst of our circumstances that is the sacrifice.

Taking Every Thought Captive

May your whole spirit, soul, and body be preserved complete, without blame...

1 Thessalonians 5:23 NASB

I shared with a church prayer group that our prayers will not "avail" anything on Sunday, if we are not taking thoughts captive throughout the week. In James 5:16, it says, "The earnest (heartfelt, continued) prayer of a righteous man (woman) makes tremendous power available (dynamic in its working)."

When do prayers *not* avail much? According to Hannah Hurnard, author of *God's Transmitters,* "when our transmitter is clogged."

When our thoughts are thoughts of anger, jealousy, or unforgiveness – our prayers become ineffective. "Every thought should be holy, that is, separated from all that is antagonistic to holy love. All our thoughts are to be alive with the love of God. For it is really true that all thought is either creative or destructive, and is going forth from our minds into the vast universe of the realm of thought, then our thoughts are more lasting and powerful in their effects than our words and deeds can ever be (Hurnard)."

Jesus said that to hate someone was equal to murder and to lust after someone was equal to adultery. The Bible says to "take every thought captive" (2 Corinthians 10:5), and we are told to have "the mind of Christ" (1 Peter 4:1).

1 John 1:7 says to "walk in the light as He is in the light." To walk in the light, we must yield every negative, unbelieving, angry, or lustful thought over to the Lord.

My pastor refers to this process as "keeping the fish tank clean." Allowing too much algae to build up on the glass and in the water "clouds" our lives and eventually leads to death. He teaches that the greatest filtration system for our lives is the Word of God. When we hold our life up to His Word, the Holy Spirit brings us into alignment and into the cleansing of the Lord's forgiveness.

God says, "If there is anything worthy of praise – fix your MINDS on it.

Walking in the Spirit means taking every thought, word, or action captive unto the Mind of Christ.

Courage to Face Ourselves

When He was alone with His own disciples, He explained everything.
Mark 4:34

I have come to the conclusion after over 35 years of serving the Lord and 20 years in the marketplace with co-workers and managers, the most difficult thing for humans to do is to examine their own souls. The fear of exposure of our weaknesses and the desire to continually look good externally, prevents us from moving forward with God's purpose for our life.

For some people it is pride, for others ignorance, but for me it was always embarrassment that I was still not measuring up to God's expectations. I grew to realize that Jesus comes with GRACE to deliver us, not to condemn us.

In 1976, I had read in Revelation 2:26, "He who overcomes, he who keeps my deeds until the end, to Him I will give authority over the nations." I wrote in my Bible "Lord, some day I will be a ruler in Jesus' kingdom. Give me the qualities of a good ruler. In Jesus' name. Amen."

I knew, even then, as a baby Christian, I wanted to be a leader for God. In 1985, God called me to leadership and confirmed to me that it was my destiny. In 1996, after many failures, I began to realize what a long journey of preparation I was on.

In my journal on September 26, 1996, I wrote, "I am beginning to take the calling and responsibility of leadership more seriously than ever before. I embrace the training and preparation, and I am more patient with the length of time it is taking. My long road of humility and suffering has purged much from me, and I continue to be refined for your work. I feel I will never measure up, but I know with You, all things are possible."

I tell my students that our time on earth is a tiny dot on the timeline of our lives. What we learn on earth, we will take into all eternity. Recently a friend shared Malachi 3:3 with me: "He will sit as a refiner and purifier of silver, and He will purify the priest, the sons of Levi, and refine them like gold and silver, that they may offer to the Lord offerings in righteousness."

My friend told a story of a woman who asked a silversmith, "How do you know when the silver is purified, and how long do you hold it in the fire?"

He replied, "Until I see my image in the silver."

Do not be afraid to get alone with God and examine your soul for any impurities. It is much easier to give them to Him now than to wait for Him to turn up the fire.

Be encouraged today. If Jesus is the Lord of your life and your plans are yielded to Him, you are exactly where you need to be. The fulfillment of the vision is in His hands.

The time between the promise and fulfillment of the vision is the testing. In Habakkuk 2:3, God says, "If it (the vision) seems slow in coming, wait. It's on its way. It will come right on time" (Msg).

Abiding

I am the true vine, and My Father is the Vinedresser. Any branch in Me that does not bear fruit (that stops bearing) He cuts away. I am the Vine; you are the branches. Whoever lives in Me and I in him bears much (abundant) fruit. However, cut apart from Me (cut off vital union with me) you can do nothing. When you bear (produce) much fruit, my Father is honored and glorified, and you shall show and prove yourselves to be true followers of Mine.

John 15:1-2, 5, 8

With multiple responsibilities in today's busy world, we are all looking for peace, strength, wisdom, love, confidence, and orderliness. I believe these are fruits that result from abiding in the Lord.

The opposite of these gifts from God are stress, worry, fear, anxiety, insecurity, confusion, weakness, sickness, anger, frustration, hopelessness, and more. The story of the vineyard tells us that these energy robbers are not what flow through the vine to nourish us or to help us achieve God's purpose for our life.

A study of the word abiding reveals the kind of abiding relationship God wants us to have with Him:

Continuous – persistent, holding on, pursuing, remaining, going forward inch-by-inch;
Enduring – tolerating, longsuffering, patient, waiting;
Dwelling – sitting down in quiet, sitting still;
Expectant – hoping, trusting;
Waiting –expecting, gathering together, patiently anticipating.

And what are the promises when we abide in the Lord? In Isaiah 40:31, the promises are strength, power, not being weary or tired, able to run tirelessly, being close to God, and having vigor to endure.

In Psalm 23, the promises are restoration, provision, guidance, love, comfort, friendship, protection, hope, home, healing, rest, peace, God's presence, and fearing no evil. In Psalm 91, the promises are stability, shelter, refuge, deliverance, covering, satisfied, shield, answered prayer, long life, and assigned angels.

God says we are His sons and daughters – we are grafted in to His vine now, and He flows through us. "You are (sons and daughters); and if (sons and daughters), then heir(s) through God." (Galatians 4:7).

"He who did not withhold or spare (even) His own Son but gave Him up us for us all, will He not also with Him freely and graciously give us all (other) things?" (Romans 8:32).

What are some practical ways to abide? Remain faithful and do not give up or run away. Love and forgive people. Be patient and tolerant of one another. Pray in all things.

Worship the Lord and read His letters to you in the Bible. Talk to Him, make time for Him, and listen. Fellowship with others and let them minister to you.

Corrie ten Boom, Holocaust survivor said, "If you look at the world – you'll be distressed. If you look within, you'll be depressed. But if you look at Christ, you'll be at rest!"

Fresh or Stale?

Jesus answered and said to him, "Most assuredly, I say to you, unless one is born again, he cannot see the kingdom of God."

John 3:3 NKJV

Often when we prepare our "to do lists" for the week we can develop the Monday morning "blues" – especially if we just had a great weekend. Can you relate? Whenever my assignments become an effort and not a joy, I know it is time to bow my head before the Father to bring the freshness of the Spirit back into my life.

I often sit in my car in the parking lot of my workplace in prayer until there is more of Him and less of me. I always begin with thanking Him for my job, for providing me with income and prospering the work of my hands, and for giving me the skills, talents, and wisdom that I can use in the world.

I often add, "Lord, I need confirmation today in the midst of all these tasks that there is a spiritual reason for me to be here and that this job is part of Your plan for my spiritual life, not just my physical life." I spend time with Him until I feel His peace and strength.

On one such morning, within that same hour I received a call to meet a client that I had talked to on the phone but never met. On the way to the appointment, the Spirit of the Lord spoke to my heart and said, "I am going to confirm to you that this person is a Christian."

By the end of the appointment, the client asked me if I was a Christian, and we spent several minutes encouraging each other with the joy of discovering that we both were believers. I then added this person to my *Marketplace Christians* devotions list as a leader I needed to pray for in our community. It was such a simple answer to a big prayer, but I returned to work with the joy of the Lord knowing that His destiny in my life is to encourage believers and leaders in the marketplace.

Bruce Wilkinson was inspired to write the book *Secrets of the Vine* because of staleness in his own life. Once he focused less on what he could do for God and spent more time with God, he began to bear fruit in his life.

I have two of his powerful statements written in my journal: "Unless your friendship with God becomes your first priority, you will never fulfill your true destiny as a Christian or a leader," and "His purpose is not that you will do more for him but that you will choose to be more with Him."

Jesus said, "I am the vine and you are the branches. He who abides in Me, and I in him, bears much fruit, for without me you can do nothing" (John 15:5, NKJV).

I close today's devotion with this Scripture, Ephesians 6:10: "Be strong in the Lord (be empowered through your union with Him); draw your strength from Him (that strength which His boundless might provides)." Thank you, God, for all the exciting spiritual things you have for us in the marketplace.

Leave Room for God

But when it pleased God…

Galatians 1:15 NKJV

Are you a multi-tasker or at least trying to be? If you make room for God, you can expect Him to show up in surprising ways in the midst of your meetings, your presentations, your preaching, your teaching, your projects and your plans. There is no mountain in your work life or ministry that God is not big enough to overcome.

I continue to be inspired by God's concern over the details of my job. I have seen His hand upon so many assignments and challenges. He is the master coordinator of our affairs if we will give him a chance to come into our schedules.

Bruce Wilkinson in the devotional book *The Prayer of Jabez*, asks, "What overwhelms you today? What is the goal you feel incapable of completing? Draw a small picture or symbol of it in a box. Write its name inside the box, too. Then draw a wide circle around your box to represent God. He is greater; He surrounds your challenge. Then pray over your drawing until you accept in your deepest heart that God is bigger than any opportunity or any obstacle."

For seven years, I managed an major annual foreign policy event where 500 people attended lectures over the course eight weeks. One year, the professor who we paid to coordinate and moderate suddenly stepped down.

With God's presence in my life, I immediately chose not to panic and to commit the entire challenge into the Lord's hands. I even contacted some people to pray for me.

At first, I felt a little ashamed asking for prayer for a work request since it may seem minor to other people. God knew, however, it was major to me, and He was faithful to respond.

I left room for Him to create what the event should look like, and I began to make phone calls and do research on the internet to find presenters for eight current world topics. God gave me favor, and one-by-one people came into my life, supported me, found other contacts, and helped me to be successful.

One example of the miracle God did for me was trying to find an expert in Southern California on "Sudan and the War in Darfur" (Africa). My research, through government agencies in Los Angeles (the closest big city) and through the Anti-Defamation League, confirmed there was only one expert on this topic. He was a crisis consultant, lived in Washington, D.C, and was currently visiting Sudan several times a year.

In faith, I contacted him and he agreed to speak. He arrived in Washington D.C. from Sudan one week before the event, flew to my community to present, and flew back to Africa two days later.

God did not want just anyone – he wanted the best! I stayed within budget during that crisis AND God gave increased revenue of $12,000! He helped me beyond my expectations!

The other impact this experience had on my life was in discovering the atrocities going on in this country. Husbands were being murdered and women were being raped. I began to pray for this country and asked others to do so. In 2006, our government began to respond to help the people of this country.

Invite God into your projects and leave room for surprises. Noted 19th century clergyman and author, Phillips Brooks said, "Do not pray for tasks equal to your powers. Pray for powers equal to your tasks."

Producing Grapes for Jesus

"I am the vine, you are the branches. He who abides in me, and I in him, bears much fruit; for without Me, you can do nothing."
John 15:5

How do we abide? We need to spend more time with our Lord in prayer and in His Word. I like to refer to abiding as "Jesus plus nothing."

We cannot do anything of ourselves to produce grapes. Only Jesus can produce the grapes if we plug in to Him – the Vine. However, abiding does take some effort in prayer and reading the Word.

Gloria Copeland of Kenneth Copeland Ministries confirms this: "Abiding in Jesus isn't something that comes automatically to any believer. It's a lifestyle that involves discipline and effort. We have to choose to give ourselves to our union with Him, to give Him first place where our attention is concerned. If we want to grow spiritually, if we want to walk in power and in fellowship with the Lord, we'll have to spend the time it takes to know Him."

The more responsibility we have in the marketplace, the less time we seem to have to abide. Men and women constantly ask me, "How can we possibly do it all?"

To produce "much fruit" for God as the Bible instructs, seems impossible. But God said that if He calls us to do it, He will enable us, and that the burden will be light.

There is only when possible way to produce an abundant harvest for God – let Him do it through us. Spend time with Him instead of time trying to figure it out or worrying.

Ephesians 6:10 summed it up best: "Be strong in the Lord (be empowered through YOUR UNION with Him); draw your strength from Him (that strength which His boundless might provides)."

Work Life Balance

"Come to Me..."

Matthew 11:28 NKJV

One of the "hot" leadership topics of this age for employees is to have work life balance. Corporate America's idea of work life balance is putting on-sight exercise rooms in their offices, dry cleaning services in the lobby, and Starbucks stations on every floor.

Their intentions are to reduce stress while increasing productivity, but when push comes to shove, most companies today would be pleased if you canceled your vacation with your family and gave your time to the good of profitability for the business.

Finding work life balance is our responsibility, not corporate America's. God not only encourages physical rest from our work activities, He wants us to be in a spiritual rest. He wants us to have undisturbed peace of mind.

There are many things that can separate us from God when we are under stress and pressure. We may avoid a discussion with Him by staying involved in busy work, we may sleep to avoid the pain, or we may talk to friends who are going to sympathize with us instead of give us spiritual counsel.

If we succumb to things that separate us from God, it will sap our strength and slow our spiritual growth, because it is splitting us from the One that can give us the strength and wisdom we need. In Matthew 11:28 Jesus says, "Come to Me, all you who labor and are heavy-laden and overburdened, and I will cause you to rest. (I will ease and relieve and refresh your souls.)"

When I go to bed exhausted, with problems on my heart or mind still unresolved, and the busyness of the day has kept me from spending time with Him, I pray for sleep and peace and set my alarm to wake up one hour early, so I can spend my first 30 to 60 minutes with Him. I lay everything at His feet until He is carrying my burden, and I am refreshed to start a new day.

If the anxiety tries to come back throughout the day, then I take a short walk, talk to Him, and breathe in His presence. David, the psalmist sang, "Early in the morning will I rise up and seek Him."

God understands the need for rest. He created a day of rest – a holy day set apart from Him. He knew at the creation of man and woman, that they would need to rest in order to have long life and survive. Enter His rest and a peaceful state of mind today.

It's Time

He who dwells in the secret place of the Most High shall remain stable and fixed under the shadow of the Almighty...

Psalm 91: 1

Since the mid-1990's, the Lord has given me a vision of grapes. I cannot stop thinking about them. I have grape paintings in my living room, grapes on my dining room table, and grapes on my charm bracelet. Along with the vision came the words, "It's Time."

When I looked up references to grapes in the Bible, it always referred to "crushing." Of course, I kept telling myself "it's time for the harvest" or "it's time to develop the fruits of the Spirit," not crushing!

Now I realize that the last ten years have been a time of "crushing" to make me into the wine that God needed to pour out to His children. Without the pruning , the vine will only produce leaves, not fruit.

What circumstances did God use to squeeze me? Difficult managers, jobs that did not value me, people that didn't love me, the loss of several pets, fear of not having enough money, and being stretched to the max with responsibility and schoolwork. Sound familiar?

My calling is leadership. Over and over I have "crushing" experiences that are forming my management skills.

I have a friend who is studying to be a counselor. Over and over again, the Lord gives her opportunity to practice interpersonal and conflict resolution skills. The pressure has a purpose – to cause us to pour out a refreshing new drink.

Brothers and sisters, I truly believe that "It's Time" also means that the end is drawing near. There is a great crushing happening in the world and people are facing great pressures with earthquakes, hurricanes, job loss, and family deaths. If we face these things in our own life with the grace of God and let Him mold us, we will be able to pour ourselves out to others and give them the love of Jesus Christ in their crushing times.

Don't be caught off guard, keep your candle lit, and be prepared in maturity and strength. Yield to Him in the crushing of the grapes and receive with joy His hand upon your life.

What did King David do in one of the most crushing times of his life? When he almost lost his life to the Philistines who wanted revenge for the death of Goliath, he escaped into a cave and sang these words: "I will bless the Lord at ALL times; His praise shall continually be in my mouth. My life makes its boast in the Lord; let the humble and afflicted hear AND BE GLAD. O magnify the Lord with me, and let us exalt His name together" (Psalm 34: 1-3).

Blessed Are the Unnoticed

Blessed are the poor in spirit…

Matthew 5:3 NASB

"Blessed are the poor in spirit," is from the *Sermon on the Mount.* It is saying that when we recognize that we our paupers, and we cannot get into heaven on our own merits, we are blessed. When we realize that we are poor in spirit, we recognize we are worthless without God and are able to accept what Jesus did for us.

We enter the kingdom of heaven because of Jesus, not because our excellence or works. The poor in spirit are the ones who "will see God."

The same is true of our service here on earth. Sometimes the invisible and unnoticed can do more for God than the popular and dynamic.

When God called me to leadership at a national level through the American Parents Association, I thought I would always be "out front" doing exciting things for Him. For the past sixteen years, God had me behind the scenes. I was "second in command" or the "right hand" of various managers in multiple organizations, but never completely in charge.

I was in a constant state of waiting for the great leadership position to happen again, but it never did. As I reflected back on my job opportunities, I discovered that I was able to do more for God behind the scenes than I realized, because I had the freedom to minister to God's children in the marketplace.

At Hewlett-Packard, I met with a sister-in-the-Lord at least three times a week during lunch hour to pray. We walked around the boxes of inkjet printers, praying for our families, the company, and the nation.

As a college faculty member, I am able to be the advisor for the student Christian Club. I was privileged to encourage future Christian leaders who I believe are called to the nation and to the world.

God has a huge purpose for the invisible and unnoticed – and sometimes, in my case – the un-promoted. God has given me just enough leadership authority to have the freedom and the flexibility of my work hours to encourage others or pray for their needs.

Multiple times I have prayed for Christians in the parking lots of where I have been employed. I have walked with them in times of pressure, crisis, or rejection.

I shared with a close friend, "I feel like a stealth airplane. I swoop in, say a prayer, and swoop out. I never know if I have made an impact for God or not."

The dramatic change of going from speaking in front of 600 government leaders in the 1980's to praying for a Christian in the college parking lot has not always been easy, but I have learned, it is just as powerful. My friend responded to my comments by telling me she talked to a woman who knew me 20 years ago.

She shared, "Wendy gave me a word from the Lord, and it changed my life forever. Till this very day, I have kept that word in my heart." She went on to say that it influenced how she prayed for her children. Today, both her sons serve God in the ministry. One is a pastor who has used a couple of my *Marketplace Christians* daily devotions in his sermons.

When my friend shared this with me, I wept at the thought that one stealth pilot visit into this mother's life, a moment I barely recall, may have made more of an impact on the kingdom of God than the message I shared with 600 government leaders.

Jesus the Leader

You call Me Teacher and Lord; and you are right, for so I am.
John 13:13 NASB

In the "Industrial Age" following World War II, the concept of managers serving others was considered an oxymoron. After all, leaders must have power, authority, and title to make people submit, obey, and be productive.

Yet, Jesus never demanded that His followers submit to Him – they submitted out of freewill and personal choice. Immediately preceding this statement confirming that Jesus is our Teacher and Lord, He had just finished washing the disciples' feet and said in verse 14: "If I then, your Lord and Master, have washed your feet; ye also ought to wash one another's feet" (KJV).

Trying to apply this concept in the business world is a challenge, especially with deadlines, competition, and productivity goals. Leaders must get their work done through others, and extensive research over the past sixty years has evaluated what managerial methods work best.

Jesus could have been a taskmaster, but He never would have had any real authority. John Whitmore, author of *Coaching for Performance,* writes: "Building others' self-belief demands that we release the desire to control them or to maintain their belief in our superior abilities. One of the best things we can do for them is to assist them in surpassing us."

Jesus' style of leadership was definitely that of coach, mentor, educator, and developer. Once He got into people's hearts, they wanted to follow Him and obey Him. "In industry, you can only move with the hearts and minds" (Whitmore).

It takes a great deal of time to coach and mentor employees with a goal towards wanting to develop them and prepare them for better opportunities. It also takes a great deal of patience when they do not respond. We can only give our best - the results are in God's hands.

What is important is that we treat others the way we want to be treated. We must have faith to believe that Jesus' management style served Him well, and therefore today, it will serve others well, serve us well, and serve the company well.

Jesus was the greatest CEO in the universe, and we need to use His leadership style above all others.

Internal Anchors

...the simplicity that is in Christ.

2 Corinthians 11: 3 KJV

Jesus knew how to make things clear in times of spiritual confusion. He held on to His internal anchors of what He knew God told Him to do.

Laurie Beth Jones, author of *Jesus CEO,* says, "He didn't come unglued when John the Baptist began to doubt him. He didn't care whether Caesar smiled or frowned." Jesus sought his approval from God, not from people.

In the marketplace, we just keep doing the right things that we know to be true in our heart, and the simplicity of Christ's love will shine through us. Jones calls this being an "Omega leader that has a backbone like a rod of steel."

I have a unique leadership style. In fact, a leadership test I took said that my style was shared by less than 1% of the population. When I measured my leadership ability by this test, I went into spiritual confusion. I began to doubt God's calling on my life to be a leader.

When I studied all the different methods and styles of leadership and management and compared them to me, I became more confused, and I doubted who I was and who God was calling me to be. One morning I asked in prayer, "Lord, how do I know if I am a true leader if no one ever tells me I am a leader?"

I went to my computer, and the first e-mail message I received was from a personal career coach and professor, "Wendy, you are a leader in your heart and soul."

I knew God was saying, "Trust your internal anchors, and just let the simplicity of Christ shine through." From that moment forward, I decided to just appreciate the unique "1%" leader God made in me and to allow Him to work through His creation.

Once I perceived God's will in my spirit and decided to just obey what He called me to do, my heart and mind became still. When challenges came my way, I continued to operate in the stillness and the confidence of the Lord, using those internal anchors He had given me.

Don't Be A Clog

*Strip yourselves of your former nature (put off and discard your old
unrenewed self), which characterized your previous manner of life and
becomes corrupt through lust and desires that spring from delusion; and be
constantly renewed in the spirit of your mind (having a fresh mental and
spiritual attitude), and put on the new nature.*

Ephesians 4:22-24

Have you ever seen the posters "No Whiners Allowed?" I think that
we whine in our circumstances more than we should, and it grieves the
Holy Spirit.

We must spend less time complaining about where God has us and
more time trusting, praising, and thanking Him. Otherwise we become a
hindrance to His plan – a "clog" that blocks the flow of God through us.

Jesus said, "The kingdom of God is at hand." That means when we
take Jesus into our workplace, His kingdom is right there with us. As we
thank Him for our boss and the employees that surround us and as we
thank him for the job He has given us, the kingdom of God can operate
in that place and bring prosperity and blessing to all.

I like to imagine that I have angels assigned to me, and they come to
work with me. If I am whining or complaining, it ties their hands from
operating on my behalf, or at the least, they must be very uncomfortable
in my presence.

When I am trusting and praising God, they are empowered to work
on my behalf and rejoicing right along with me. I don't want to wait until
I get to heaven to be in the midst of rejoicing angels. I want heaven on
earth surrounding me right now!

I am not saying that I do not have days that I wish I were somewhere
else or working in a different situation. When I go through those stages in
my life, I review my journals, writings, and mission statement and see
where I am with the vision and plan I believe He has for me.

I work on some things in the evening or weekend that bring me closer
to that vision. It helps me to see that my job is just one step of the overall
plan He has for my life. To help focus on the vision rather than the

present situation, pray this prayer:

> *Lord, I think you that you had a plan for me while I was still in my mother's womb. You have designed everyday, and before the world was created You saw this day, and this situation as part of Your plan for my life I rejoice in this day that You created. I thank You for my life. I thank You for the gifts and talents You have given me. Show me how I can be used by You today as I wait for complete fulfillment of the vision. Help me to not clog this vessel with complaining. I receive peace and direction from You now in my circumstances. In Jesus' name. Amen.*

After this devotion went out by E-mail, I received this message from a friend in Washington state: "You may already know this but I find your choice of the word "clog" interesting. The French word for clog (the wooden shoe) is sabot. When the dutch factory workers went on strike they threw their "sabot" into the machinery to make it stop, hence the word "sabotage". So by putting a clog in the way of the Lord, you are committing "sabotage" on yourself!"

Part 7
Leadership Skills

Picking up the Towel

Now that I, your Lord and Teacher, have washed your feet, you also should wash one another's feet.

John 12:14

This is a message about the daily tasks in our lives. Sometimes I think, "When I am the leader of my own organization, I'm going to do it 'this way.'"

God says, "I want you to do it 'this way' now." He wants us to pick up the towel, wash feet, and serve others in menial tasks right where we are. How we serve today is an indication of how we will lead tomorrow.

I like being a leader more than a manager. A leader gets to inspire, create vision, and be a change agent. A manager has to manage operations, budgets and the conflicts of people. After a challenging week of problem solving, I drove home one evening and said, "I don't want to do this Lord – I don't enjoy it. I just want to move on to greater things."

Do you know what He said in my spirit immediately? "Grow up." Honest! He said, "Grow up and face your responsibilities. You cannot be a leader without being a manager. There will always be seasons of these tasks, challenges and pressures. If you can't handle this – you are not going to be able to handle the next step I have for you."

I now receive my challenges as training gifts from God. Our mundane tasks and responsibilities are God's training ground in our lives. He engineers them to get us ready. Are you embracing your gifts? Jesus called it "picking up the towel."

Inside each of us is a "knower" that just knows the right thing to do. Once it is clear in your "knower" that you are called for a certain purpose, task, project, marriage, ministry, or job, REST in knowing that He will help you achieve your goals. May the FORCE OF GOD be with you.

Transformational Leadership

And Jesus took with Him Peter and James and John, and brought them up on a high mountain by themselves. And He was transfigured before them.
Mark 9:2 NASB

When Jesus was transfigured He "became resplendent with divine brightness and His garments became glistening, intensely white" (Mark 9: 2-3). At the mountain, Jesus talked with Elijah and Moses and they named the place, "the Mount of Transfiguration."

Later at the ascension, Jesus said that He would go to the Father so that He could send the Holy Spirit. He wanted us to have access to the same transformational power He walked in.

It is interesting that one of the most recent leadership theories in organizations is referred to as transformational leadership. As we transfer from the task-orientation of the Industrial Age and rapidly move into the change-orientation of the Information Age, people-centered and team-centered strategies of management are found to be the most effective.

Transformational leadership has also been called charismatic leadership, inspirational leadership and symbolic leadership. This type of leadership goes beyond ordinary expectations by transmitting a sense of mission and inspiring new ways of thinking. Because of rapid change and chaotic environments, transformational leaders are vital to the success of business (and of churches).

The characteristics of a transformational leader remind me of Jesus – the greatest leader to ever walk the face of the earth: trusting one's subordinates, developing vision, keeping cool, encouraging risk, being an expert, inviting debate, and simplifying things.

At the Mount of Transfiguration, Jesus spent time with His Father and met with Moses and Elijah, both great leaders, to be clear on God's plan for His life. He then spent every waking moment pursuing the vision God had given him and using a transformational leadership style, inspiring others to do the same.

There are two critical messages here. We need to go to the Father, and we need to go to others we trust for council.

God never expected us to lead and make decisions alone. Jesus created access to the Father, so that we can go and receive the plan and direction He has for our lives. If we spend time with His transformational love and power, we will witness a transfiguration in our own lives.

With God or For God?

Not that we are fit…of ourselves to…count anything as coming from us, but our power and ability and sufficiency are from God. (It is He) Who has qualified us (making us to be fit and worthy and sufficient) as ministers and dispensers of a new covenant (of salvation) through Christ…

2 Corinthians 3: 5-6

It is actually easier to serve God with works than to believe God will work through us in the things we cannot do. This spiritual experience of exercising your faith will remind you that God will not forsake you, and He will provide you with all that you need for the situation at hand. Being with God is recognizing, that apart from Him and his grace, we are nothing.

God sometimes gives us assignments that we do not feel adequate enough to accomplish. "I know that nothing good dwells in me" (Romans 7:18, NASB). However, we are qualified because of God.

Why? Because the Christian training ground is all about letting God work through us as we work with Him. Know this – the people on the receiving end will get an anointed touch from God in addition to your gifts and talents.

Many people ask me, "Where do you get the energy and the time to do what you do?" Primarily it comes by walking with God, rather than doing things for God. Work in itself will exhaust you, but carrying God's burden is light.

God told Ezekiel to prophesy to the dry bones by saying, "Thus says the Lord God to these bones: Behold, I will cause breath and spirit to enter you, and you shall live …and you shall realize that I am the Lord…(Who calls forth loyalty and obedient service)" (Ezekiel 37:5-6).

Energy, peace, and strength come from walking in the knowledge that everything we are, everything we do and everything we have is by the grace of God.

Are your bones dry and tired right now? Come into His presence, acknowledge His grace and mercy, and allow His living Word to breathe life into your bones. Dwell in Him, and He will dwell in you.

"God said, I will dwell in and with and among them and will walk in and with and among them, and I will be their God, and they shall be My people" (2 Corinthians 6:16).

Levels of Leadership

…be perfect, just as your Father in heaven is perfect.
Matthew 5:48 NIV

Jesus was talking about perfection in the way we love people in this passage of Scripture. He was instructing us to not let our likes or dislikes rule our Christian life and love of others. "If we walk in the light as He himself is in the light, we have fellowship with one another" (1 John 1:7, NASB).

When it comes to loving others, we are not to be a good person, or a good Christian, but be like God Himself – perfect. We are to show the other person what God has shown us – unconditional love.

John C. Maxwell in *Leadership 101,* says there are various levels of leadership. In Level I, you are aware of the history of the organization, you accept responsibility, you do your job with consistent excellence, and you do more than expected.

In Level II, you process a genuine love for people, you make those who work with you more successful, you see through other people's eyes, love people more than procedures, influence others in your journey, and deal wisely with difficult people.

Maxwell says this level must be mastered before you can advance to Level III, which is where change, profit, respect, results, and productivity take place. Every time you change jobs, you begin at Level I.

There are also "Stages of a Team." Teams move from "Forming" to "Storming" to "Norming" to "Performing." Until relationships are built in the first stage and conflicts worked out in the storming stage, the team is not going to be productive.

I recently took a diversity class. The content taught five levels of tolerance. Two of the top three – "Acceptance" (differences do not really matter to you) and "Tolerance" (you treat with respect, but you are uncomfortable) – seem like positive behaviors.

That is until you read what true diversity appreciation is: "This rating means that you see their differences as positives. You consider them to be smart, talented, or funny; or possessing traits, skills, or attitudes you value. In the workplace, you enjoy being around these people. In fact, you choose to be around them."

Until we can love "perfectly" in situations He brings our way, we will not move on to the next "level" with Him or with His plan for our lives. If I get "stuck" in the journey – I stop, reflect, and see if there is someone I am not loving, releasing, or empowering the way my Father in heaven would. The goal is to manage others the way we want to be managed – in the love and grace of God.

Beware of Energy Leaks

So if when you are offering your gift at the altar you there remember that your brother has any (grievances) against you, leave your gift at the altar and go. First make peace with your brother, and then come back and present your gift.

Matthew 5:23- 24

In business and industry training, we give several different personality, communication, and motivation inventory assessments. Most of them score how you behave or communicate "under normal circumstances" and how you behave or communicate "under stress."

The problem is, in the 21st century workplace, we are all under constant stress and pressure – it's never ending – and we tend to be more tense, serious, and frustrated in the stressful times. The best thing to do is to admit it, and confess it to God.

When you offend someone, apologize and reconcile. This is especially true for leaders because it will create "energy leaks," and you will not be able to manage effectively.

One of my favorite books, *Jesus CEO,* by Laurie Beth Jones, asks the question "how many energy leaks do we have in our own daily lives?" Leaks like angry words, distractions, gossiping, coarse words or jokes, worry, stress, or agitation. These things will deplete your energy and your ability to walk in the Spirit of the Lord and cause you to be temperamental with your co-workers.

How can we keep the positive energy in our lives? Spend more time in prayer, praise God for the good things in your life, have quiet time in the middle of the day, and as soon as the Holy Spirit gently warns you about a negative thought or action, yield it over to the Lord and ask for forgiveness, allowing Jesus "to have his perfect work in you."

The Smallest Detail

If you…remember that your brother has any (grievances) against you …
Matthew 5:23

The Lord is saying, "Before you come to the altar with your offering, your worship, or your religious activities, first go to your fellow man." We cannot move forward with the things of God until offenses are resolved. When I feel "stuck" in my spiritual walk, I go to my prayer closet and meditate on all the people in my life and past circumstances to see if there is someone I need to forgive or if I need to ask forgiveness of someone.

About a year ago, I remembered a disagreement I had with another Christian school board member. The Lord revealed to me that she was right and that I was wrong. I called her and reminded her of the incident and asked her to forgive me.

She said, "That was so long ago, it doesn't matter."

I replied, "It did matter regarding my relationship with my God and I needed her to forgive me." She said she forgave me and I felt released. Since then we have been in communication.

John Maxwell writes, "Religious busyness often tramples right over human need. Formalism, ritualism, and institutionalism can drive religious machinery right over hurting, needy people, all in the name of religion itself."

When you come to the altar with your gift, Jesus will ask, "What did you give to mankind today?" Maxwell believes, "You will never truly live if you do not daily connect with the reality of your fellow man."

Those smallest details that God may be talking to you about could be an unwillingness to get out of your comfortable circle of friends, traditional schedule, or fear of people who are different. When we arrive in heaven and Jesus says, "Well done my good and faithful servant," I believe it will be the small details we do for Him that He will be referring to.

Walking in God's Stride

Little children, keep yourselves from idols (false gods)—(from anything and everything that would occupy the place in your heart due to God, from any sort of substitute for Him that would take first place in your life).
1 John 5:21

When God adds one more responsibility to my "basket," I sometimes think, "There is no way God intended us to do so much. We need to go back to the 18th century when people did far less and in fact did nothing after sunset."

In 2005, I visited Colonial Williamsburg, Virginia. It depicts the original lifestyle of 18th century Americans. I learned that those citizens had to go 50 miles to get a wagon of wood for heat and cooking, and they did not go to Target to purchase all their goods – they made them! Add to that the Revolutionary War in their backyards, and I would say the stress was equivalent, if not more to what we have now.

I tell my students that after sleeping and eating, there are only 100 hours left in a week for activities. Forty percent of those hours are work related. You have 60 hours to get everything else done, including family responsibilities, home repairs, car maintenance, church, exercise, relaxation (including television), and devotion time with God.

The students have to figure out where they are going to put "going back to school" in this schedule. I tell them, if God called them to get their degrees, then God knows the master plan to get everything done.

Time belongs to God. However, we need to make sure ALL the things we are doing are in God's will for our lives, and learn how to walk with God in His stride, not ours.

Often we become impatient waiting on God's plan for our life, so we get busy with other activities that "look like" what we are supposed to be doing. Other times we get into God's calling and are overwhelmed with the responsibilities and the challenges.

The reason it is a challenge is because God wants you to lean on Him the whole time. He wants you to make Him your burden bearer as you carry out your duties.

God said to Habakkuk: "Look around you among the nations and see! And be astonished! Astounded! For I am putting into effect a work in your days (such) that you would not believe it if it were told you" (Habakkuk 1:5).

That is what God is doing in us today – He is getting us ready for future days that will astound us, but they will not move us because we are prepared.

What is the practical application of all this? Evaluate your life, and see if there are any "busy activities" that God did not call you to and let go. Do not pick up any more, and WAIT until God directs you.

Follow the peace of your heart. If you lose your peace, get back on track until you have it back again.

When the load seems too heavy, quit analyzing it with your intellect. Rather, stop, pray, and let your spirit get in the stride of God, trusting His ability to complete His work through you. You will learn that you can survive the 21st century walking in God's stride, not your own.

A Point Person

According to my earnest expectation and hope, that I will not be put to shame in anything, but that with all boldness, Christ will even now, as always, be exalted in my body, whether by life or by death.

Philippians 1:20 NASB

When I take time to reflect on my past, I am tempted to "be ashamed" of my failures. I then recall that it is all about Jesus and His life in me, and I can see how much He has developed and matured me through the years, because of my complete dependence on Him. He then encourages me to not give up and to continue to run the race.

I ask myself, "Why do I keep running this race when I continue to not measure up?" The only answer I can give is because I am forgiven of so much, and when I look at what Jesus did for me – I want to not only follow Him, I want to obey Him and please Him.

His love sacrifice for me makes me want to sacrifice my life for Him. In 2 Corinthians 5:14, we read, "For the love of Christ controls and urges and impels us..."

When I stand before the Father on judgment day, I want to know for all eternity that I did my best, and that in spite of my mistakes, my heart motive was always toward God. "For we must all appear and be revealed as we are before the judgment seat of Christ, so that each one may receive (his pay) according to what he has done in the body, whether good or evil (consider what his purpose and motive have been, and what he has achieved, been busy with, and given himself and his attention to accomplishing)" (2 Corinthians 5:10).

Several people have told me that they see me as a "point person." A point person is someone at the very head of a triangular military formation.

The person at the head takes the full force of the battle receiving attacks on the left, right, and center. Next to that person is a banner-bearer. For me, the banner is a banner of victory with the name of "Jesus" written on it.

As lonely and vulnerable as the point person can be, it is comforting for me to know that behind me is a whole army of Christians that I am encouraging and leading into victory with me. If I give my all in writing these devotions, sharing over 35 years of battles and victories, perhaps others will receive courage to be a point person for the army God is calling him or her to lead.

The Justice of God

As they led Him away, they ceased one Simon of Cyrene...and laid on him the cross made him carry it behind Jesus.

Luke 23:26

Many people consider Simon in this Scripture verse and think, "Why did he deserve that assignment to carry the cross of Christ? He was just a bystander, minding his own business and he had to carry the cross of Christ in front of all those people." Others might say, "That was not fair."

What God requires you to do may upset other people's plans. If they ridicule you, will you continue to obey and pay the price, or will you crumble under the pressure?

In a Christian university class I teach on principles of management, we often discuss doing justice in business. The book *Business Through the Eyes of Faith,* by R.C. Chewning leaves no rock unturned regarding our responsibility as business owners, managers, or employees.

Chewning asks the question, "If there was potential to make a great deal of money manufacturing dangerous chemicals using Cambodian refuges who are eager for work and will work at a lower wage, would you do it?"

He replies to his scenario by saying, "Biblical justice refers to the way relationships are structured so that there are no built-in disadvantages to any individual or group of people" (Chewning).

Justice reflects God's character, and we must reflect His character in the workplace by making just decisions. We may not be subject to making a major decision about manufacturing chemicals, but we are faced with daily decisions of obedience that may impact other people's lives.

For example, I once worked with an all male telephone crew as a PBX Telephone Installer (and yes, pole climber) in the 1970's. We were given 10 to 12 work assignments per day. Using the work ethic God intends us to have, I worked diligently and rapidly to complete all 12 assignments by the end of the day. My more seasoned and experienced co-workers were bringing 2 or 3 back to carry over to the next day.

One evening, three of the men (strong union guys) took me aside and told me to stop completing my orders "or else." They said, "If we all worked like that, we would work ourselves out of jobs." It was very intimidating, and it did not help that they hated the fact that a young female was doing "their job." I had to make a choice.

Should I do what God required of me, or what men require of me, even if my obedience causes some degree of "suffering?" I decided to obey God and serve my employer "as unto the Lord" leaving the justice of the situation in His hands.

We serve a just God. If we walk in justice and mercy, He will show us justice and mercy.

Let Your Yes Be Yes

Samuel was afraid to tell Eli the vision.

1 Samuel 3:15 NKJV

Samuel, a youth, had to tell his elder Eli, a priest in the temple, that Eli was in sin and that the nation was in danger. It is difficult to be obedient to God when you have to give bad news or you have to say something that makes people uncomfortable. That is what the mission of the prophets is – they are truth-bearers.

An organization that understands this to the fullest is Alcoholics Anonymous. They know that the truth is what will save someone's life and care more about that person than the hurt feelings or anger that will be expressed because of the truth. Dr. James Dobson, Christian psychologist and radio host, calls it "tough love."

God is teaching me that good leaders do not hold back or avoid the truth. They speak the truth in love.

Samuel had to do what was best for the nation, and managers often have to do what is best for the organization. Tough love may be painful to facilitate or participate in, but other employees will be grateful for your tough leadership choices that in the end benefit everyone.

Abdication or waiting for things to correct themselves is not good leadership. Imagine Joseph and Daniel, who interpreted kings' dreams, in risk of death!

Trying to please others is not God's will – obedience to Him is always the best choice. When Apostle Paul received a most unusual message from God regarding ministering to the Gentiles, as well as to the Jews, he said, "I did not immediately confer with flesh and blood…" (Galatians 1:16, NKJV).

I asked a successful CEO, "What one piece of advice would you give me?"

He replied, "Be honest with people. Don't put flowers in front of it, and flowers at the end of it. Just speak the truth in kindness, and do what you know to be the right thing."

Another leader told me, "God says let your 'yes' be 'yes' and your 'no' be 'no.' There is no middle ground with God." Good advice.

Part 8
Gifts and Talents

In God's Grip

I press on to take hold of that for which Christ Jesus for which Christ Jesus took hold of me.

Philippians 3:12 NIV

When God chooses a preacher and lays hold of him or her in a supernatural way they "hear the call." He or she usually does not question whether they are suited for the job or not – they just answer the call.

Even though we are all called to share our testimony and testify to the truth of God, I would estimate that more than 90 percent of Christians are "called" to the workplace or home – not to preaching. I believe that God has laid hold of each one of us also for His purpose, and our jobs and careers have been carefully designed for us.

Just like Apostle Paul, we need to "press on toward the goal to win the prize for which God has called (us) heavenward in Christ Jesus" (Philippians 3:13-14, NIV).

Marketplace Christians can choose to prayerfully determine and evaluate if they are in the career that God selected for them. If they are not, they need to continue their education and prepare for their calling. After acknowledging and accepting the gifts and talents He gives us (which usually align with the calling), we then can accept the training ground He provides for us.

At times it may seem that the assignment is beyond our ability. But when we sense God's grip on us and know it is His calling, we can also know that He will equip us with everything we need to complete the task.

Allow Him to give you more skill and more ability in the challenges ahead and learn how to rely on Him in those times. When He opens a door for you, step through into His Grace and continue to run the race He created for you.

Many Christian workers and college students have told me they feel like "second class citizens" in their churches because they are not in full-time ministry. I encourage them by sharing that marketplace ministry is a high and challenging calling, and I remind them of Daniel, Joseph, Esther, Nehemiah, and David - leaders in the Bible who served in government and community.

More credit and encouragement need to be given to workplace Christians (including stay-at-home parents) and their efforts to let God's light shine in the world among the non-believers. At the same time, marketplace Christians and church leaders should work together to discover how marketplace gifts and talents can contribute to the church.

Become A Lifelong Learner

Do not be conformed to this world, but be transformed by the renewing of your mind, so that you may prove what the will of God is, that which is good and acceptable and perfect.

Romans 12: 2

I enjoy teaching college students the topic of problem solving. Workplace problems that were shared by the class became an opportunity for creative solutions and an expectation for God to give us wisdom and direction.

I shared with the students a motivational message from Dr. Norman Vincent Peal, "When you see a problem coming down the road, holler 'Hello, Problem! Where have you been? I've been training for you all of my life!'"

Author Laurie Beth Jones calls Jesus a "Turnaround Specialist." In every situation His job was to turn things around, and there was no set formula – He did something unique and different every time.

God wants to take you somewhere you have never been before. He wants you to be a lifelong learner. Read something you never read before, visit someone you never visited before, try something you never tried before, love someone you never loved before, give something you never gave before, and discern something that God wants you to do that you have never discerned before.

Not sure where to start? You can start with Romans Chapter 12.

Discover what your gift is (verses 6 – 8), begin to share your gift in the church and in the marketplace (with prayerful direction), and live in love according to the remaining verses (9 - 21).

Guaranteed, you will begin to have a sense of a spiritual destiny for your life.

His Capacity, Not Ours

Have not I commanded you? Be strong and courageous. Do not be terrified; do not be discouraged, for the Lord your God will be with you wherever you go.
Joshua 1:9

Even though the Lord assures us that He will not give us more than we can endure, there are still times we will say, "God, this is more than I can handle. Surely this cannot be Your will." When we tell God that His demand on us is out of proportion to the gifts He gave us, we are accusing God of not knowing what He is doing and saying that He desires us to be vulnerable and unable to cope.

In contrast, Apostle Paul rejoiced in his weaknesses, because through his weakness, God could be strong. Paul proclaimed, "I can do all things through Christ who strengthens me!" (Philippians 4:13, NASB)

God has repeatedly demonstrated in my life that He prefers to use me in areas where I do not have experience or education so that I must completely depend on Him. I can give Him the glory when His ability is manifested through me. He even prefers to give us words "in that same hour" so that it is His thoughts and not a planned presentation.

I recall a time when I was campaigning for a school board position. I was a young mother struggling to overcome fear on a daily basis. I thought I was way over my head and that surely God had made a mistake in picking me. He always showed up just when I needed Him and demonstrated HIS GIFTS through me in amazing ways.

His presence was especially strong on candidate debate nights with hundreds of people watching. The Lord was faithful to give me His wisdom and answers in that same hour.

One man commented to my husband, "When the enemy is at his worst, Wendy is at her best. The more vicious the attacks, the more anointed her response."

My husband knew all my insecurities and all my inabilities. He would simply respond, "It's God."

The next time God gives you an assignment that you think you are not capable of, remember it is probably the perfect assignment for your skill because God will be able to complete His perfect work through you.

The Valley Below

Jesus took with Him Peter and James and John and led them up on a high mountain apart by themselves. And He was transfigured before them and became resplendent with divine brightness.

Mark 9:2

One of my favorite books is *Hinds' Feet on High Places* by Hannah Hurnard. It's based on Psalm 18:33: "He makes my feet like hinds' feet (able to stand firmly or make progress on the dangerous heights of testing and trouble); He sets me securely upon my high places."

In the story, the main character is *Much Afraid*. She is a crippled child who loved her Good Shepherd and was often mocked and ridiculed by the people in the village. She lived a life of pain and rejection.

The Good Shepherd invited her to the mountain's high places above the village so that she could receive "mountain goat feet" that could take her anywhere and enable her to overcome anything. He gives her "escorts" called *Sorrow* and *Suffering;* and when she makes it to the top after a long courageous journey, she is transformed into *Grace and Glory* and is no longer *Much Afraid.*

I relate to *Much Afraid* because I had polio as a child and limped in pain for several years. I also relate to her mountain top experience with the Good Shepherd, Jesus, because I had a beautiful mountain top experience when I received Him in my heart as my personal Savior. Like her, I could live in His presence forever, in the glory of His transforming power and love.

Much to my surprise, when I read the sequel to the book, *Mountains and Spices,* Jesus gave *Grace and Glory* a new message: "You must go back to the village down into the valley below, back to the people who hurt and rejected you, because they need Me." The story is one of the most powerful teachings on following Jesus.

Jesus took Peter, James, and John to the high mountain, but eventually they had to go back to the valley below to pour themselves out to others. What does it take to go down into the valley? Compassion.

Matthew 9:36, speaks about the compassion of Jesus: "But when He saw the multitudes, He was moved with compassion for them, because they were weary, and scattered, like sheep having no shepherd" (NKJV).

Are you lacking compassion? Good. That means you can ask God to fill you with **His**. If Jesus lives in your heart, it's already there, just call upon Him. Pour out your compassion to someone in the valley below today.

Faith Tested and Tried

"Without faith it is impossible to please God . . ."

Hebrews 11:6

Faith is a very personal gift. The Bible says that as we use our faith, our portion of faith increases; and if we lack faith, we should ask for it: "I believe, Lord, help my unbelief."

When we go through a test or trial, we have a tendency to spend a lot of hours in worry, fear, whining, complaining, questioning, and avoiding. The sooner we activate our faith in the situation; the sooner all lessons will be learned and spiritual growth will take place.

My husband and I took a spiritual gifts test. We both scored high in "Faith."

We later discussed, "So what does that mean?" For both of us it seemed that the gift of faith is primarily for personal circumstances in our lives – not necessarily something we would give to others. I cannot make someone else have faith or give them my faith – they have to exercise and grow their own faith.

We then realized that a large portion of faith did not come with the "package" of salvation when we were born again. We received a very small portion and began to use it in God-designed circumstances.

After over 30 years of walking in faith, we recognize that the gift had grown because of tests and trials; in most cases, those challenges were a gift from God. I went back to the spiritual gifts test and looked at the statements regarding faith:

I have an unswerving confidence that God will keep His promises in spite of apparent evidence to the contrary.

I have received from God an unusual assurance that He will do the impossible to fulfill a special task.

I am able to trust God implicitly in every area of my life and give Him the opportunity to work out His purposes as He chooses.

I accept God's promises at face value and apply them to given situations without doubt.

How does our gift of faith become a blessing in other people's lives? By sharing with others from confident experience.

My husband and I both believe through faith that God will save a marriage that appears to be over. God will bring back a child that appears to be lost. God will take care of your family when he calls you to a special task away from home.

God will give you a home when the bank says they will not. God will give you a job when others take it away. God will give you a revelation in your spirit, through His Word, or through others, that He is going to bring victory in a specific situation.

Faith is believing with your heart His message – not what your eyes see or your head tells you. We have discovered that whatever we have gone through, others who had gone through it before us were there to encourage us. For others who are going through problems now, we are there to encourage them.

Most important - faith in our tests pleases God. It is the stuff that makes "good and faithful servants."

Mustard Seed Faith

If you have faith as a mustard seed...nothing will be impossible for you.
Matthew 17:20

In the Bible, James was a man who faced problems straight on with the Word of God. He encouraged people to quit talking the talk and start walking the walk.

In James 1:3-4, James writes: "Count it all joy when you fall into various trials, knowing that the testing of your faith produces patience. But let patience have its perfect work, that you may be perfect and complete, lacking nothing" (NKJV)

Like a mustard seed growing into a beautiful huge tree, our faith grows with each experience. God builds our faith precept upon precept. God wants to bring the promises and the vision into our lives, but if we do not step out in faith, the supernatural power of God is not going to come forth. In order to have a harvest, there has to be a planting.

As soon as we believe God's promises, the enemy comes and tries to discourage us and steal the seeds (the promises of God), but we must remain assured of God's character – He will not forsake us. Jesus was very clear about the seeds falling on good soil and bad soil, and how they are vulnerable to the wind if not watered, or how the weeds and cares of the world can choke out the crop.

God has planted a seed of faith in your life. He has told you that He has a job for you, He has a vision for you, He has a plan for you, He has a spouse for you, He has a home for you, He has a ministry for you, or He has supernatural wisdom and strength for you.

Do not be discouraged. Do not let the cares, worries, or fears of the world choke out that promise. Do not let any more time pass without watering that seed that God planted in your heart.

Water it with praise and thanksgiving. Nourish it with the Word of God. Strengthen it by fellowshipping with others (who believe in you), and WRITE IT DOWN, and meditate on it.

God told Habakkuk, "For the vision is yet for an appointed time and it hastens to the end (fulfillment); it will not deceive or disappoint. Though it tarry, wait (earnestly) for it, because it will surely come; it will not be behindhand on its appointed day." (Habakkuk 2: 2).

The reason God seems distant is because He does not want you to be an elementary school child anymore. He wants your test to become a testimony of His faithfulness. He wants you to have "university faith" and become a professor of His promises.

Some of you could not step out, so God forced you out of your comfort zone. You feel lost, abandoned, and alone.

In order for God to take you from the natural to the supernatural, He had to bring you to this place. In order for the vision to be fulfilled, He had to bring you to a place where you have to trust Him. He wants you to know, that the faith you are standing on right now is a firmer foundation than the world's security that you had.

No man can stop what God has for you. No company can take away the plans God has for you. No business or government controls the destiny that God has for you. You only need a tiny seed of faith to blow the enemy out of the water and discover that nothing is impossible for our Great God.

Blessed Are the Poor in Skills

Roll your works upon the Lord (commit and trust them wholly to Him; He will cause your thoughts to become agreeable to His will, and) so shall your plans be established and succeed.

Proverbs 16:3

I used to think that the message of Jesus, "Blessed are the poor for theirs is the kingdom of heaven," meant that some day the poor would be rich in heaven – or those who suffer now will be blessed later. I believe it also means, "Blessed are the poor in spirit for they shall receive Jesus."

Those that are spiritually hungry, know they need God; they search for Him and shall find Him. Those that are satisfied and believe they do not need God, will not find Him. We cannot be spiritually rich – inherit the kingdom of heaven – until we are spiritually destitute.

Even though the Lord has given me some gifts in leadership, I do not excel in management, especially in finance and accounting. I keep asking him why He puts me out on the front lines of management when I would be perfectly content behind the lines in the classroom or writing.

He does it because I am "hungry" in this area, and I crave for Him to work through me. I know I am deficient, so I have to depend on Him.

Almost every step I take is with dependence on the Holy Spirit. My challenges become opportunities to teach students in the Christian university that learning management skills is necessary, but depending on God's guidance is powerful.

If God has called you, He will equip you. Are you poor in your experience and abilities on your job right now? Rejoice! In your weakness God gets to be strong and His wisdom will prevail.

We Are One

…that they may be one, just as We are one…

John 17:22 NASB

There is a great deal of focus on personality in corporations, and psychological tests are given to help us understand our behaviors, our preferences, and our motivations. We think we can understand the great depths about ourselves, but in reality, only our Creator can fully understand who we are.

Jesus always talked in terms of "we" rather than "I". He was closely connected to the Father throughout His entire earthly journey and frequently said, "I and the Father are one" (John 10:30).

Our true identity can only be found in God. God knows things about our ability and potential that we do not even know. A wealth of talent and skill may have been kept beneath the surface, because we allowed people and parents to mold the image we have of ourselves.

My father repeatedly inferred that I was stupid, and so I believed that I was. It wasn't until I was 44 years old that I discovered I was smart enough to get a 4.0 GPA in college.

Ask yourself the question, "If I had no fear, what would I be or what would I do with my life?" Bruce Wilkinson, author of *The Dream Giver,* calls people that keep you from "crossing over" to fulfill your dreams *border bullies.* I think we have *border bullies* in our head – messages of limitation and self-defeat.

I sometimes laugh when I realize I am a college professor. I say, "God, I did not know I would like doing this. I never saw myself as a teacher. I did not even know this about myself."

God replies, "I always knew."

Is there something that God knows about you, but you have never asked, because you are happy in your comfort zone? Ask God to show you EVERYTHING He created you to be.

Pray this simple prayer, "God, you are the potter and I am the clay. Break me, make me, and mold me, into all You want me to be. Reveal to me the gifts You want me to use. Show me for what purpose You created me. In Jesus' Name. Amen."

Bypass Your Intellect

No one can come to Me unless the Father who sent Me draws him…
John 6:44 NIV

When I was delivered from being a 4th generation Christian Scientist, a battle between my mind and my spirit took place. The Holy Spirit was calling me to go down to the church altar and ask for forgiveness, but my "mind" was arguing with me using Christian Science teachings such as, "If you are created in the image and likeness of God how can you have any sin that needs to be forgiven?"

I had to follow my heart and the drawing of God, and I quickly walked to the front of the church where I met my Savior. He enveloped me during that communion service with messages of love and forgiveness, transforming me in that moment.

I had to take the first step toward God. I had to will myself to the church altar and overcome the lies of Satan in my mind.

Walking a life of faith is exactly the same. When God stirs in our hearts to love and forgive someone, to visit someone in prison, to call someone on the phone and encourage him or her, to let go of something, to confess a sin, what is your immediate response? Does your mind begin to argue with your heart? Do you start to rationalize that you cannot do that?

If you are holding back, you are missing out on awesome experiences with God. Additionally, the Lord cannot trust you to do His will, and you will hear His voice less and less. If you obey even the smallest little direction, God's direction for your life will become clearer. The life of obedience is a life of joy.

It will always take a step of faith to follow God's leading, just as it did when you got saved, but it may start with a battle in your mind. Jesus said in Matthew 11:12, "The kingdom of heaven has endured violent assault, and violent men seize it by force (as a precious prize—a share in the heavenly kingdom is sought with most ardent zeal and intense exertion)."

There is nothing passive about that statement. Do not sit and wait for God to do something extraordinary in your life. Instead, ask Him, "What little thing can I do for You today?"

Then bypass your intellect if it doesn't make sense, step out in faith and do it! You will then watch the extraordinary take place. Go with God. And He will go with you.

Part 9
Workplace Witness

The Gift of Faith

Do you believe this?

John 11: 26

Jesus told Martha that her brother was going to live again and asked her "Do you believe this?" She believed that Jesus could have healed him if he had arrived before he died; she believed Jesus had a personal relationship with God and that God would listen to Him, and she even believed "You are the Christ."

Jesus wanted to know in these overwhelming circumstances, "But do you believe?" He wanted her to have an intimate relationship of faith with the Father.

It is tempting to depend on others who have greater faith and active prayer lives. It is also tempting for people of great faith to enjoy the esteem of others looking to them for prayer and answers to their problems.

God has trained me to hold back my prayers of faith when He is strengthening someone in their own personal relationship with Him. I could easily become a hindrance to His work if I exercised my faith and did not help my brother or sister grow in theirs.

I usually ask, "What are you believing for?" I then encourage him or her to pray along those lines or I pray an agreement prayer. AGREEMENT is the key. Unless God gives me a "word of knowledge" for the impossible or for a miracle, I simply encourage them in their faith.

The Bible says we are all given a portion of faith. If we use it, it grows. If we do not use it, it depletes. God brings us to places where we have to step out in faith and completely trust Him.

Each time, we realize that He truly can provide for us, open doors for us, turn things around for us and protect us. When you come face-to-face with Jesus in prayer as Martha did, and He tells you "only believe," hold on to the hope that all things are possible with Him.

Seeing the Light

And Saul said, "Who are You, Lord?" And He said, "I am Jesus..."
Acts 9:5

On the road to Damascus, the light of Christ blinded Saul, a Roman citizen who was known for persecuting Christians. When Saul repented, he was renamed Paul by Jesus, and he became a devoted bondservant of the Lord.

Unless an unbeliever recognizes that there is a higher authority, the explanation of salvation will make no difference to him or her. In fact, if you give someone the information before they are ready to acknowledge Jesus Christ as Lord, you risk interfering with God's perfect timing and doing spiritual damage.

When Saul saw the light, he was on his way to arrest Christians. Scripture states that it makes no difference what sin you are in when you come to the light, but "woe is me if I refuse the light" (John 3:19-21).

The Bible says that no man comes to God unless the Holy Spirit draws him. We must work in partnership with the Holy Spirit.

Let your light shine, do acts of kindness, share your testimony when appropriate, and plant seeds. When a person is ready to acknowledge that there is a higher power, the soil of their heart will be ready for the planting. Sometimes it is necessary for people to have the soil of their hearts tilled for a long time before they are ready to have the light of Jesus revealed.

My grandmother was a staunch Christian Scientist. Christian Scientists believe Jesus was a good teacher, but they do not recognize Him as the Son of God. They also do not believe in sin, heaven, or hell, so they see no need for salvation. My grandmother was a good religious person, but she would harden her heart and clinch her jaw if I shared the Gospel.

I continued to plant seeds and allowed the Holy Spirit to water them with a great deal of prayer. On her death bed, at age 82, in the hospital in her weakest hour, I said, "Grandma, Jesus loves you."

With tears in her eyes, her response was, "Oh Dearie, do you think

He ever could love me?" My heart rejoiced!

She acknowledged that there was a Lord, that His name was Jesus, and that she needed His love and forgiveness. She was asking if the King of all Kings could ever forgive her. She was acknowledging her sin and a need for a higher power to accept her. It was no longer based on her good works, but on grace.

I quickly explained how easy it was for her to accept Jesus into her heart and accept His forgiveness. She was too weak to pray, so I prayed for her as I held her hand, hoping with all my heart that she was agreeing with me.

She squeezed my hand, smiled, and there was a peace on her face. A few months after she died, I had a dream about her that confirmed that she was with Jesus.

In my dream on Christmas Eve, I was asking her to stay for the family celebration and begged her not to leave. She said, "Oh Deary, I have a bigger celebration to go to than this."

Do not give up praying for your loved ones, friends, and co-workers. It will all be in God's timing for them to see the light.

Jesus Was A Radical

Greater love has no one than this that one lay down his life for his friends. You are My friends if you do what I command you.

John 15: 13-14 NASB

In the Master's degree program at Washington State University, I was required to study Tibetan Buddhism as a philosophy. I saw it as an opportunity to compare and contrast it to my own Christian faith.

Buddhism is taught as a religion of love and self-sacrifice. However, when you study it closely, the central reason for sacrifice is so that you may find self-enlightenment.

Buddhists are all seeking "a perfect state of mind" (nirvana), and yet it is always elusive to them. Even if a Buddhist claims to find Nirvana, what does that do for mankind? I think self-enlightenment can be a selfish and self-centered pursuit.

In contrast, Christianity is a letting go of self. Jesus asks us to lay down our lives for Him by laying down our lives for others and then receive nothing in return.

The teachings of Jesus have many contradictions that the world finds hard to accept. "Give so that you might receive but not as the world gives," "lay down your life so that you may gain your life," "give everything to the poor and follow me," "he who is the greatest must be the least," "if they ask for your shirt, give them your coat," and the list goes on.

Why are these actions so important? Because "they will know we are Christians by our love."

Followers of Christianity are often accused of being wimps that have to use a crutch to get through life. The truth is, Jesus was a radical, and it takes a great deal of courage to follow Him.

There is nothing wimpy about it! Being a Christian means a lifetime of pouring out to others, being faithful and obedient, and facing persecution.

Jesus would call "nirvana" when you can love your enemies, give them the shirt off of your back, and pray for them.

A Little Bit of Sin

And if your right hand causes you to sin, cut it off and cast it from you; for it is more profitable for you that one of your members perish, than for your whole body to be cast into hell.

Matthew 5:30 NKJV

In this verse Jesus is talking more about the destructive force of sin that will lead you into hell than he is about cutting off body parts. However, I have felt "maimed" over the years wondering if there would ever be an end to the things I was doing wrong as God continued to "cut" more and more flesh off of my life.

Why does He challenge new believers with so many restrictions? It is because even "a little bit of sin" will destroy us.

I think Daniel recognized this at age 14, when he refused to eat the king's food in captivity. Surely other Israelites must have thought, "What's the big deal?"

When King Darius established the decree that for thirty days people could only worship the king and not any other god or man, most people probably just remained quiet for 30 days or went into their "prayer closets." Certainly the lion's den was not worth a few prayers to God.

Daniel, however, continued to pray to his God three times a day in his bedroom window, facing the East as he had always done, visible to any passerby. For Daniel, there was no compromise, and no little sin was worth being cut off from God.

God's discipline is not easy, but in the end it reaps great rewards. Look at the faithfulness of God on Daniel's behalf.

I was greatly impressed by a message given by an international evangelist in the 1970's who said, "Twenty to thirty years from now, there will be such a great shaking on this earth and such a great compromise of moral values, that the only Christians who will survive will be those grounded in the Word of God. The ONLY thing that will survive the great shaking and confusion will be the Word of God."

I have held on to that all these years determined to not allow the pressures of "Daniel haters" to cause me to compromise. We must keep yielding to the Holy Spirit and keep standing on His Word, refusing to be moved by any pressure or thing that rises itself up against our Lord.

At the same time, we must balance this message and not use the restrictions that God places in our life to criticize someone else. We are all being pruned at a different rate, so we need not judge others, lest we be judged. I say in true humility, "but for the grace of God I go."

I Was Blind

You must be born again.

John 3:7 NIV

In John 3:3, Jesus said, "No one can see the kingdom of God unless he is born again" (NIV).

I was raised a fourth-generation Christian Scientist. Christian Scientists do not believe that Jesus is the Son of God, and they do not believe in heaven or hell.

Even though I read the Bible as a child and a young adult, I could not see the truth about salvation in the Scripture. I was blind. When I repented and received Jesus as my Savior, the Scriptures became clear to me.

People often ask me how to witness to people of false religions. I can tell you two powerful things. First, when people used the name "Jesus," it rocked my boat. There was something provoking and stirring in my soul when His name was mentioned. The name of Jesus pierces the flesh and sheds light in the darkness.

When you discuss your faith even in a casual conversation, use the name of Jesus, the Name above all names, rather than Father or God, and you will see results. Remember, even the false religions say Father and God with ease.

Secondly, people of false religions do not have peace. They have a form of spirituality or positive thinking, but deep down inside, there is still a huge vacant hole that can only be filled with Jesus.

It is important that you express and demonstrate that peace in whatever way you can, because eventually, unbelievers have to admit that they do not have what you have. There are a lot of imitations for joy, but you cannot copy peace.

Ken Blanchard, author of *The One Minute Manager, Situational Leadership, and Servant Leadership,* shared his salvation story at the 2005 Leadership Summit in Costa Mesa, California. Blanchard was not a Christian for the majority of his consulting and public speaking career.

He was a humanitarian and opposed the concept of "sinners." He believed that people were basically good.

Blanchard told of Bill Hybels, senior pastor of Willow Creek Community Church in South Barrington, Illinois and author of *Courageous Leadership,* sharing a powerful statement with Ken. Hybels said, "Imagine if we had to be good to get into heaven and on a scale of 1 to 100, only 100 could get you in. Mother Theresa may have been a 95, and you may be a 75, but it is Jesus who fills in the gap for you and gets you in."

Knowing that Jesus filled in his missing gap rather than having to admit he was a terrible sinful man was the key that opened Ken's heart to Christianity. He is now a powerful witness for Christ.

Jesus always carefully worked His way through a crowd, sharing God's love. We must be flexible and open to the unique and individual ways that Jesus wants to use to remove the scales off of someone's eyes, and we also must be willing to share what Jesus means to us when asked. It only took a couple of faithful saints to rock my boat so that Jesus could open my eyes.

Proclaim the Good News

And (pray) also for me, that (freedom of) utterance may be given me, that I may open my mouth to proclaim boldly the mystery of the good news (the Gospel.)

Ephesians 6: 19

It is always so tempting for me to share with a non-believer my salvation experience and stop short of sharing the good news of Jesus Christ. When I was saved, I had to face God and realize that I was unworthy and needed Jesus Christ.

Even though witnessing makes most of us uncomfortable, it is simply placing before people the truth about our separation from God and the good news of how we can be reconnected with Him through Jesus. Witnessing can begin with our own personal testimony, but it has to end with the truth of the good news of what Jesus did on the cross, and people must be pointed to the purpose of the cross. Jesus said, "If I be lifted up, I will draw all men unto me."

Opportunities to witness may be limited, but if you pray with expectation, God will open some doors. The question is, in the one small window of opportunity you are given, are you prepared to share as briefly and concisely as possible the truth about who Jesus is and what He did?

The first time someone witnessed to me she pierced my heart with the question, "Who do you think Jesus is?" I did not have an answer.

She then proceeded to tell me who Jesus was – a story I had never heard before. It rocked my boat!

The truth pierced the darkness all around me and the mention of the name of Jesus shook something within me. She had demonstrated love, kindness, and friendship up to that moment, but when the moment came, she did not hold back the truth.

A friend recently shared with me, "It says that at Pentecost power came from on high so that they could BE bold witnesses. I'm not ready to witness verbally yet, but I'm working on the BE part of it – living a moral life before God and being a Christian witness in my actions that unbelievers can see."

She is also on the right track. Before we tell others about God, we better make sure we are a LIVING WITNESS first.

Pass it Forward

Study to show thyself approved unto God... rightly dividing the word of truth.

2 Timothy 2:15 KJV

There is a movie about a boy who experiments with doing good things for people and then telling them to pass it forward by doing something good for someone else. The good deeds are multiplied throughout the community, and lives are changed.

In the Christian community, even our challenging circumstances need to be passed forward to strengthen others. God says, "Confess your faults one to another that you might be healed."

It is not always easy to share in these devotions the experiences where God has tested me, refined me, and disciplined me. But through it all, He has always increased my faith. I believe that our testimony of God's victory defeats Satan's power in our lives.

No matter how difficult it is to express what God is doing or how vulnerable it makes us feel, we must pass on God's revelation to others. When we do, two things will happen: 1) We will be strengthened in the truth God taught us; and 2) Our faith will become the strengthening for someone else.

These expressions of God's truth in our lives come from the experiences of the winepress of God where the grapes are crushed. I used to think that God's lessons in my life were never-ending, that the time of training and preparation for His promises in my life would go on forever, and that I would never measure up to the task He had for me.

Then I read *Secrets of the Vine* by Bruce Wilkinson and understood what the crushing and waiting was all about when he shared the story of King David. King David must have grown weary also. He was anointed King of Israel, but he had to go through one battle and trial after another before he was actually crowned.

Wilkinson points out that this "pruning season" for David was necessary to prepare him, and that God was "not trying to take away, but faithfully at work to make room to bear more fruit and add strength, productivity, and spiritual power." James 1:3-4 says, "Knowing that the testing of your faith produces endurance. And let endurance have its perfect result, so that you may be perfect and complete, lacking in nothing" (James 1:3-4).

Psalm 66:10,12: "For you, O God, tested us; You refined us like silver…but you brought us to a place of abundance" (NIV). I now thank God for all the trials He victoriously brought me through, so that I can share them with others that they may be strengthened.

"Thank you Holy Spirit for bringing to mind, God's promises, God's testing times, and God's victories in our lives, and give us the boldness to share them with others. Amen."

Experiences

We have received...the spirit which is of God; that we might know the things that are freely given to us of God.

1 Corinthians 2:12 KJV

On the front cover of a Bible I received for Christmas in 1986 as a gift from my husband, I wrote a quote by evangelist Eugene Peterson, "There is a great market for religious experience in our world; there is little enthusiasm for the patient acquisition of virtue, little inclination to sign up for a long apprenticeship in what earlier generations of Christians called holiness." Below it, I wrote my own personal thought: "Steadfastness and lifelong training are better than quick religious experiences."

The Lord has blessed me with many spiritual experiences and revelation knowledge over the past 35 years, and I have always strived to humbly focus on the source – Jesus. I am careful to put my faith in Him and His Word, not the experiences.

Immediately after I was born-again and delivered from the bondage of a false religion, I had one revelation experience after another. Because Jesus had broken the stronghold that the false religion had on my life, He became my close teacher and friend, communicating with me very clearly every day and showing me truth in the Scriptures.

After three years of this extraordinary training and infilling of the Holy Spirit, He spoke to my heart and asked, "If you never experience Me like this again, will you still follow me? Will forgiveness and a promised home in heaven be enough for you?"

I anguished over that question because I knew when I said, "Yes, Lord, I will follow you no matter what," the experiences I was having would diminish, and He would take me into a wilderness of training and preparation. After many anguished minutes of tears, I told Jesus, "Yes," and I made Jesus Christ the Lord of my experiences.

My experiences did not produce salvation and redemption in my life, Jesus did. My experiences are not worth anything unless they give Jesus Christ the glory.

The Lord has asked me to share my experiences with others to give them hope and encouragement. I share them with others at the risk of some thinking I boast. But I boast not of myself – for I am a wretch, a forgiven sinner – I only boast of the God of my faith who does glorious things for us all. My faith is in God and in His Word, not in my experiences.

In a new Bible I received in June 2004 as a PhD graduation gift, I wrote, "Jesus said, 'Blessed...are those who hear the Word of God and obey it" (Luke 11:28, NIV).

The Courage to Follow

Jesus answered him "Where I am going you cannot follow Me now, but you shall follow Me afterward."

John 13:36 NKJV

Peter told Jesus he would follow Him even unto death. However, Jesus predicted that Peter would not have the courage and that he would deny Christ and even curse His name. It was not until Peter received the Holy Spirit at Pentecost that he had the power from on High to lay down his life for his Lord.

Many Christians are at first excited to receive "a ticket to heaven" and to know the Lord's forgiveness on earth. It usually takes another crossroad to make Him the Lord of their lives.

I receive courage to follow Jesus when I read His words to His disciples, knowing they are also for me. Before the crucifixion, Jesus prayed to the Father, "I have manifested Your Name (I have revealed Your very Self, Your real Self) to the people whom You have given Me out of the world. They were Yours, and You gave them to Me, and they have obeyed and kept Your word" (John 17:6).

Then Jesus continues, "I am not praying (requesting) for the world, but for those You have given Me, for they belong to You. All (things that are) Mine are Yours, and all (things that are) Yours belong to Me; and I am glorified in (through) them" (John 17:9-10).

Jesus tells the Father that He has given us the glory and honor that He received from God. Why? "That the world may know and (definitely) recognize that You sent Me and that You have loved them (even) as You have loved Me" (John 17:23).

How can we not follow Christ? We must be faithful to continue His mission on earth – to share the good news of God's love.

In my early twenties I went door-to-door with a Campus Crusade for Christ evangelistic team. I was so nervous. We carried the *Four Spiritual Laws* booklets with us.

At this one apartment, a sweet, gray-haired lady answered the door. I said, "Hello, I was wondering if I could share with you on this beautiful Sunday how Jesus changed my life?" I got to the part where I asked, "Would you like to be assured of going to heaven?"

She responded, "I was just thinking and worrying about that this week. I've been asking God to show me. I've been a good Catholic, but I really don't know if I am going to heaven or not. Yes, I would like to know how." With tears in her eyes, she prayed the prayer of salvation.

I probably had 25 doors closed in my face that day, but that one woman, who was probably over 80 years old, was waiting for Jesus to come to her door.

It takes courage to share your faith with others. When God brings someone into your path that needs to know the Lord, Jesus will be with you as you share your heart.

What is His promise? He told the Father, "I have made Your Name known to them and revealed Your character and Your very Self, and I will continue to make (You) known, that the love which You have bestowed upon Me may be in them (felt in their hearts) and that I (Myself) may be in them" (John 17:26).

Our Lord Jesus will make God known to others through you by the power of the Holy Spirit within you. Do not be afraid as Peter was. It is not about you – it is about Jesus.

People Are Watching You

"But I, when I am lifted up from the earth, will draw all men to Myself."
John 12:32

How do we lift up the name of Jesus in the workplace? Unfortunately, some believe it means to quote the Bible to a captive audience. This approach will not only get you in trouble, it has not been very successful in drawing people to Jesus.

Losing your job does not give God the glory, and the Supreme Court has ruled that you cannot evangelize someone in the workplace against his or her will. It is okay for your co-workers to know you are a Christian, but they need to know it because of the fruits of the spirit found in Galatians 5:22-23: "love, joy, peace, patience, kindness, goodness, faithfulness, gentleness, and self-control" for "against such things there is no law (that can bring a charge)."

How do we accomplish all these wonderful interpersonal skills in our lives? The answer is by lifting up the name of Jesus in our own personal lives.

As we spend more time with Him and in His Word, we become more like Him. As we become more like Him, people at work begin to see Jesus in our lives. People will notice a life controlled by the Holy Spirit, and they will be drawn to those fruits.

I have had dozens of opportunities to share God's love through my example with co-workers, but I have only had three precious incidents in my 20-year career as a leader, where colleague said to me, "There is something different about you – what is it that motivates you?" It was in those moments that I actually got to verbally lift up my Lord and it was well timed, well received, and part of God's plan.

After many years in one organization, I did not think anyone noticed my faithfulness to be kind and patient in the midst of some tough circumstances. After I departed, one of the coworkers said, "I admire you for the way you behaved when you were treated badly, and you left as a class act. You were positive, with a smile on your face, and never said one bad thing about the organization or leadership to anyone. I have so much admiration and respect for what you did."

While I worked for that organization, I had no idea that my positive attitude, words and behavior were noticed by anyone, but my behavior opened a door for a closer relationship and perhaps one day, to share with her from Whom I derive my strength.

Galatians 5:25, concludes: "If we live by the (Holy) Spirit, let us also walk by the Spirit. (If by the Holy Spirit we have our life in God, let us go forward walking in line, our conduct controlled by the Spirit)."

People are watching you. Your EXAMPLE can be the greatest lifting up of Jesus on the face of the earth – for your co-workers, your children, your friends, your students, and your family.

The Road to Damascus

I have appeared to you for this purpose...

Acts 26:16 NKJV

The most dramatic conversion in the Bible was when Jesus appeared to Saul on the road to Damascus and turned him from a Christian-killer into a fearless evangelist and renamed him Paul. Paul himself wrote, "For I determined not to know anything among you except Jesus Christ and Him crucified" (1 Corinthians 2:2, NKJV).

Today, people who love Jesus this much are called "Jesus Freaks." But the connection that Paul had with Jesus was not just an emotional one. When Ananias prayed for Paul, he received his sight, and he was filled with the Holy Spirit (Acts 9:17). Paul carefully followed the leading of the Spirit to spread the Gospel and establish churches throughout the known world in his time.

The Bible says that Paul was "all things to all men," and though he was bold and full of the power of God, he was very wise in his witness. He was more than just "bold" – he was obedient. Because of his dramatic encounter with Jesus Christ, he was willing to do radical things in the midst of criticism, such as witnessing to the Gentiles, not just the Jews.

Perhaps there is a Saul in your life. It could be a relative that has an anti-Christ spirit that mocks the Lord or persecutes Christians. Jesus said that we are to love our enemies and pray for those who persecute us.

Behind that mask of sarcasm and resentment toward Christians is a person that needs to know Jesus, and possibly someone who is called to evangelize the world. It is not easy, but when we encounter challenging unbelievers, we must pray to see the person through the eyes of God.

The reason that Paul could reach out to sinners so willingly is because he remembered the previous sinner he was – the murderer of God's children. He knew he was nothing without his personal encounter with the LIVING Lord Jesus Christ. His desire was for all the sinners of the world to experience this same Savior.

I think this is why Jesus wants us to visit the prisoners. He wants us to see them through the eyes of God. Paul is a great example of the mercy of God and a reminder that even if we fail or fall, we need to get back up and continue down that road to the destiny and purpose that God has for us in His kingdom. Today, there is someone reading this message that God wants to tell, "Don't look back and don't give up. I accept you and I love you."

Born Again of the Spirit

Clouds and darkness are round about Him...

Psalm 97:2

Some people would say there is a fine line between religion and relationship with God. I say there is a huge mountain.

I attended Sunday school, read my Bible and was raised in a good home with moral values, but I could not see or know God, because I was raised in a false religion.

Why was it false? It did not introduce me to Jesus Christ as my Savior. Until I repented of my sins and acknowledged Him as Lord, I could not see His truth in the Scripture.

Jesus said in John 3:5, "I assure you, most solemnly I tell you, unless a man is born of water and (even) the Spirit, he cannot (ever) enter the kingdom of God."

Thomas was a follower of Jesus, but it was not until he understood who Jesus really is, that he was able to say, "My Lord and my God!" (John 20:28)

The word Lord appears 5,000 times in the Bible. When God spoke prophesies to His people throughout the book of Ezekiel, calling them to repentance (as He is today), He said repeatedly, "I the Lord God have spoken it." A footnote in the Amplified Bible in Ezekiel reads:

> *"On the basis of the fact that God uses the word Lord more often than any other important word in the Bible, the word Lord becomes the most essential term in any language for the welfare of any person. It is not enough that one knows that God is God, and that He is, for only a fool would deny that (Psalm 53:1), but God demands of every person who is to be recognized by Him that he accepts Him as Lord of his life, his Sovereign Ruler, to Whom he yields implicit obedience."*

What does this mean for us in the marketplace? That we give every area of our life over to God (our attitude, our money, our time management, our temperament, our job, our integrity), and we let Jesus live through us so that others may see Him.

In these last days people will need to know where they can go to find the Spirit of God (not religion). How will they know they can go to you? Because you have demonstrated His truth, His love, and His power to save, in your realness, your kindness, and your vulnerability during tough times. Lean on Jesus because Jesus—not religion—is the strength, joy, and wisdom of your life.

The Book of Life

Do not rejoice in this, that the spirits are subject to you but rejoice that your names are enrolled in heaven.

Luke 10:20

In Revelation 3:5, Jesus said, "He that {overcomes}, the same shall be clothed in white raiment; and I will not blot out his name out of the book of life, but I will confess his name before my Father, and before his angels" (KJV) In Luke 10:20, Jesus was trying to tell the disciples to not marvel at the miracles that were taking place through them, but to marvel at the day you will stand before God.

For on that day, Satan will try to accuse you of your sins, but God will see that your name is written in the book of life, and you will enter into heaven for all eternity. At that time, the disciples did not even realize that Jesus would die on the cross for their sins to give them access into heaven.

Miracles, healings, and deliverance from evil spirits are important, but often the purpose of these miracles with unbelievers is to help them know there is a greater power that loves them. The more important miracle is salvation through Jesus Christ and having our names written in heaven.

A friend of mine went on a trip to Mexico for her birthday. She met a couple from her hometown that needed some miracles.

My friend prayed for them, and every prayer was answered. She said, "The reason God answered the prayers so quickly for the couple is because God wanted to show them just how much He loved them."

She prayed for the healing of the husband's ear, and he was healed. She prayed for the releasing of finances that were tied up because they were out of the country, and the finances were released.

She prayed for the divine healing of their nephew's girlfriend who suddenly went into a coma. She was in intensive care and not expected to live. Within four days of praying, while they were on the trip, the girl was out of the coma and released from the hospital.

The last prayer was to find a lost credit card. When my friend met the couple in the lobby of the hotel on their last day, she was sharing with this new couple how exciting it was that God answered all their prayers.

The wife, who was now a new believer agreed, but the husband replied, "Well, except I still have not found my credit card." The wife had a salvation experience and drew closer to God because of the miracles, while the husband still doubted God's divine power.

My friend said, "I believe you will find your credit card in a place you have already looked, even though you say you have looked everywhere and through everything." Two days after they got back, they found the credit card in the husband's shorts' pocket.

Of everything shared in this story, what is the most significant work of the Lord? That the wife's name is now written in heaven.

My friend, who is praying that this woman can stay strong in the Lord with a doubting Thomas for a husband, just found out that a Christian friend of hers from her church moved into this couple's neighborhood.

God was on assignment to write one more name in the book of life, and He sent someone to continue to help in her spiritual growth. Let us rejoice over the miracles God does for His people, but let us CELEBRATE His faithfulness to chase after people and bring them into the kingdom.

If Not Now, When?

Most of the brethren have derived fresh confidence in the Lord because of my chains and are much more bold to speak and publish fearlessly the Word of God (acting with more freedom and indifference to the consequences.)
Philippians 1:14

Sometimes we look back and have sadness of what might have been. Jesus does not come with a spirit of condemnation, but rather a spirit of forgiveness, and the Lord tells us to "forget what lies behind" (Philippians 3:13).

However, there is a difference between memories that keep us on track and encourage us versus memories that bring us guilt. The memory of failed opportunities for God reminds us to step out in faith the next time He opens a door for us.

I have two vivid memories of doors God opened for me that I closed, and they can never be opened again. One was in Mississippi while visiting a friend. I was attending a Veteran's Day Ceremony in a park on a warm November day, sitting next to my friend's mother.

The Holy Spirit urged me to ask her if she knew Jesus as Her Savior. I told the Holy Spirit I would bring up the subject that evening when we visited her. That evening, we found her dead from heart failure in her home.

The second time was when the Holy Spirit urged me to make a Christmas centerpiece for my next-door neighbor, which I made and delivered the following week. One evening she came over to thank me for it and shared that she needed a heart transplant, but was not eligible, and that the doctors only gave her a few weeks to live.

I talked with her, let her vent her grief, and told her I would pray for her - but I did not take the opportunity to introduce her to Jesus Christ. I thought I would have time to visit her again and build a relationship that would lead to that, but that door was closed, because she was dead within a few days.

Both experiences devastated me, but the sorrow turned into a wonderful lesson of growth for me. A few months later, I felt an urgency regarding my oldest cousin on the East Coast.

The door of concern was opened in my heart and mind, and I had to step through. I sent him an e-mail telling him that I cared for him, that if he needs anything to call, that God loved him, and I was praying for him. I also boldly shared my personal testimony and mentioned that if he had questions about life after death, that eternal life was as easy as a single prayer, asking Jesus into your heart and acknowledging Him as Savior.

I never heard back from him and within two months he had died from a massive heart attack while at the wheel of a car. Later I found out, that in that two-month time frame, he had sought out a local pastor and met with him over coffee on a regular basis. I can only pray that I will see him in heaven and that perhaps my seed-planting was part of his destiny. Either way, I had great peace from my obedience.

I do not want to miss open doors anymore. I do not want be blind to what God is doing because of my "god" of "what will people think."

What we will lose by not being bold NOW 'in this your day' when God requires it? We lose the opportunity to step through God's open door that leads to peace and joy in Him. If not now, He asks, then when?

Personal Testimonies on MarkeplaceChristians.com

"I just read Marketplace Christians-October 11 &12. You won't believe it, but every one you have sent me, has one way or the other had something to do with what I am feeling or going through. Thank you so much for these inspirational and encouraging words. They lift my spirit up when I read them, every one of them. Thank you again."

Alva, Chino, California

"What a POWERFUL message from the Lord - one which we can all follow. Again, thank you for sharing with us and helping all of us to hear Him and understand Him. Your faithfulness is precious. It is so comforting to have a woman as a Christian professional role-model and spiritual guide - thank you for all you do in His name! Keep the words coming!"

Monica, Pottery Barn , Palm Desert, California

"Wow, you have outdone yourself with this one. I am going to print this message and have it tattooed on my forehead. Thanks for the great insights. Although I don't often respond to your daily devotions, they frequently move me. They speak to my soul in a language that transcends the written or spoken word."

In His Service. Miles, Captain, Chino Police Department

"Please keep me on the list forever, I have been forwarding your devotions to my Christian and non-Christian friends. It has been a tremendous blessing and encouragement to everyone. Some have even started asking more questions about God! So, keep them coming your writings are bringing people to understand God with easy reading devotions! You are blessed and gifted women of God!"

In his Love, Ken, Biola University Student

"Dear Wendy, Just a word of encouragement! I really enjoy your daily marketplace Christians each day. I am sure you hear this all the time, but I wanted to be sure and say thank you for your godly insights, study, and regard for scripture. Keep up the good work. I am sure you have a nice devotional book in the making that will be of great value to believers in the secular workplace and those like me working in the church."

Love in Him, Pastor Michael, Presbyterian Church

"Hello Dr. Flint, I can't tell you how much your devotionals have meant to me over the last several months, and I wish you a great and happy anniversary on them. I read them everyday. God bless you for your faithful service. I feel like I have a personal leadership trainer in my life to coach me along the way, and yes I do believe you are a leader. I greatly appreciate your sacrifice in time and personal testimonies that are given. I can sometimes relate to most of the testimonies as my own, and if God can bring you this far I know He's going to do great things for me and through me. What a blessing you are to the body of Christ."

God Bless You Richly, Elizabeth, Biola student

To receive "Workplace Wisdom" Devotions Monday through Friday,
register at **www.marketplacechristians.com**

The following books and authors are referred to in MarketplaceChristians.com devotions and played a large part in the Christian and leadership development of Dr. Flint's life:

Beyond Jabez by Bruch Wilkinson
Business Through the Eyes of Faith by R.C. Chewning, et.al
Chosen to be God's Prophet: Lessons from the Life of Samuel by Henry Blackaby
Coaching for Performance by John Whitmore
Courageous Leadership by Bill Hybels
God is my CEO by Larry Jullian
God's Transmitters by Hannah Hurnard
Good to Great by Jim Collins
Hinds Feet on High Places by Hannah Hurnard
Jesus CEO by Laurie Beth Jones
Leadership 101 by John Maxwell
Life @ Work by John Maxwell
Mountains and Spices by Hannah Hurnard
Overcoming Overload by Steve and Mary Farrar
Prayers That Avail Much by Germaine Copeland
Purpose Driven Life by Rick Warren
Reflecting His Image by K.P. Yohannan
School Boards – A Call to Action by Wendy Flint
Secrets of the Vine by Bruce Wilkinson
Seven Habits of Highly Effective People by Steven Covey
The Cross and the Switchblade by David Wilkerson
The Dream Giver by Bruce Wilkinson
The Final Quest by Rick Joyner
The Great Divorce by C.S. Lewis
The Happiest People on Earth by Demos Shakarian
The Maxwell Leadership Bible
The One Minute Manager by Ken Blanchard
The Path: Creating Your Mission Statement for Work and for Life by Laurie Beth Jones
The Prayer of Jabez by Bruce Wilkinson
There's No Such Thing as Business Ethics by John Maxwell
Waking the Dead by John Eldredge

ABOUT THE AUTHOR

Dr. Wendy J. Flint is the Senior Vice President of Marketing and Sales at Boston Reed College in Napa, California. She works out of her home offices in Palm Springs, California and Temple, Texas.

Dr. Flint was a tenured faculty member at College of the Desert in Palm Desert, California and elected two-term Chair of the Faculty Development Committee. She is the author of several books and technical manuals including, Problem-based Learning: Welcome to the Real World; School Boards – A Call to Action; Instructional Design Methods; Teaching Techniques for Adult Learners; Student Leadership Skills for the 21st Century; and Principled and Practical Leadership.

Dr. Flint is published in multiple journals on teaching techniques, online assessments and organizational leadership. She is the former President of the Evergreen School Board, Vancouver, Washington; former President of the American Parents Association, Washington D.C., former learning center manager at Hewlett-Packard's Ink Jet Printer Division (WA), former Director of Marketing for Executive Forum (WA), former Training Manager, Electric Lightwave (WA), and former Director of Continuing and Workforce Education, College of the Desert (CA).

Dr. Flint received her BA in Communications with a specialization in Training and Development from Marylhurst University in West Linn, Oregon, her Masters of Public Administration from Washington State University, and her PhD in Education with a specialization in Teaching and Learning from Capella University. She is currently working on her MBA.

Dr. Flint resides in Indio, California with her husband of almost 40 years and their three Chinese Shar-pei dogs. She has three married children and six grandchildren.

1984171

Made in the USA